MW01396362

Five Star Recipes from World Famous Hotels & Resorts

Volume I

By
Linda Lang

All Rights Reserved
Copyright © 2014, Linda Lang's Taste of Travel

Dedicated to All Lovers of Fine Cuisine
and the Great Chefs Around the World
Who Bring So Much Talent to the Table
and
All the Grand Luxury Hotels and Resorts
That are Totally Dedicated to Bringing
So Much Pleasure to Our Travels.

ACKNOWLEDGEMENTS

This book represents the contributions of not only the exceptional chefs herein but the hotels and resorts whose fine establishments provide the ultimate in luxurious ambience and attentive service.

A very special thank you goes to Mrs. Beatrice Tollman, founder and president of the Red Carnation Hotel Collection, who was named European Hotelier of the Year at the 2012 European Hospitality Awards. A consummate chef, herself, her lifelong passion for food and hospitality is reflected in her close working relationships with the chefs, to whom she has entrusted many of her own recipes, and the management staffs of the 17 hotels she personally oversees. Some of the recipes from her recent book, A LIFE IN FOOD, have been shared with us for this first volume in the LINDA LANG'S TASTE OF TRAVEL series.

Another big thank you goes to Dromoland Castle's managing director Mark Nolan and executive head chef David McCann who shared a few recipes from the DROMOLAND CASTLE COOKBOOK published in 2013. Among the many notables having dined there are President Bill Clinton, Hillary Clinton, Nelson Mandela, President George W. Bush, Robert Redford, Brooke Shields, and Bono.

To Krysten Johnson, KJ Design, a big thank you for going far and beyond in designing not only this book and its cover but our new logo. Your friendship and invaluable support are as much appreciated as your meticulous attention to detail and creative talent.

Special thanks, too, to Arnelle Kendall, Molly Ruggere, Carlyle Fairfax Smith, Dana Williams, Janine Cifelli, Charlotte Novom, Janice Frechette-Artinger, Joshua Preston, Kimberly Babcock, Carolin Meltendorf, Kait Daly, Christina McGoldrick and the many others who worked so conscientiously to obtain the detailed information necessary to produce this book. And to my good friends, Maggie Rogers, Jan Juhl, and Pat Hyduk, your continual support and encouragement carried us through many a challenging day.

We could not have done it without each and every one of you.

Cover and Interior Design: Krysten Johnson, KJ Design, KJDesign4u@aol.com
Editor: Sonia Howard

PHOTO CREDITS

Front Cover Photo: Courtesy of Blantyre
Back Cover Photos (top to bottom): Palazzo Avino, Dromoland Castle, Four Seasons Resort Maui, Red Carnation Hotel Collection, Viceroy Bali
Section Title Page Photos provided by:
Breakfast & Brunch: Red Carnation Hotel Collection
Appetizers, Soups & Salads: Red Carnation Hotel Collection
Meats: Ranch at Rock Creek
Poultry: Ballyfin Demense
Fish: Dromoland Castle
Pasta: Red Carnation Hotel Collection
Desserts: Ballyfin Demense
"Recollections" full-page photos by Linda Lang

PROPERTY AND RECIPE PHOTO CREDITS:

Provided by The Red Carnation Hotel Collection: '41, The Milestone, Acorn Inn, Chesterfield Palm Beach, The Egerton House Hotel, Hotel d'Angleterre, Summer Lodge Country House, The Montague on the Gardens, The Duke of Richmond Hotel, Chesterfield Mayfair, Ashford Castle, The Oyster Box, Bushmans Kloof, Twelve Apostles Hotel & Spa. Additional Properties/Recipe Photos provided by: **Palazzo Avino**, Ballyfin Demense, **Dromoland Castle, Four Seasons Resort Maui, Island Outpost (GoldenEye Resort),** Inn at 202 Dover/Beale, **Hotel Le Toiny, Hotel Lungarno, Ranch at Rock Creek, Regent Berlin, Terre Blanche, and Viceroy Bali.**

FOREWORD

Great food knows no boundaries, geographical or otherwise. Discovering the cuisines of the world is a continuing culinary journey enriched by every new adventure we choose in life.

For nearly 40 years, I have been fortunate to travel to many parts of the world, discovering the wealth of sights, sounds and tastes of other lands and cultures. During that time, the number of world class hotels and resorts has multiplied, offering even more luxuries and cultural experiences of new and existing destinations. And the cuisines of these magnificent properties have also evolved, becoming more daring, creative, sophisticated... their artistic presentations even more exciting to the eye, palate and one's camera lens.

I have flown the Concorde across the Atlantic while enjoying champagne and smoked salmon, traveled aboard the Orient Express from Istanbul to Paris, viewed the volcanoes and waterfalls of Hawai'i's Big Island by helicopter, drifted silently in hot air balloons over the vineyards of Burgundy, walked from west Berlin to the east through the monumental Brandenburg Gate, explored the quaint towns and ancient vineyards of Tuscany, discovered the unpopulated isles and small ports of Alaska's Inside Passage by yacht, swam in the sparkling clear azure blue lagoons of Bora Bora, and watched the spectacular Canadian countryside pass by from the dome car of a luxury train.

I began keeping a journal of my favorite experiences during those early years when I first observed teams of waiters at posh restaurants ceremoniously present each course, simultaneously lifting the dome covers from our plates with great flair. Whether such showmanship actually contributes to the enjoyment of the dish is debatable. It certainly contributes to the mood.

We hope you enjoy this premier edition of our Taste of Travel series, and if you have any recommendations for future volumes, please email me at linda@lindalangstasteoftravel.com. You can also follow our blog at www.lindalangstasteoftravel.com.

Bon Voyage & Bon Appétit!

LINDA LANG

Copyright © 2014, Linda Lang's Taste of Travel
All rights reserved.
Printed by CreateSpace, an Amazon.com Company

While every effort has been taken to present correctly and completely the recipes provided by the contributing properties and their chefs, Linda Lang, Author, and Linda Lang's Taste of Travel, Publisher, do not guarantee 100% accuracy of the information provided. The Author and Publisher do not accept responsibility for any errors, omissions or inaccuracies or for any liability or loss incurred from use the information provided herein.

All text, images, and other materials within this book are subject to the copyright and other intellectual property rights of the Publisher except where specifically credited to the original providers. These materials may not be reproduced, distributed, modified, transmitted electronically, or otherwise copied or utilized without the express written permission of the Publisher and original providers. Links to suggested websites containing additional data are for informational purposes only and are not endorsements or guarantees of any kind whatsoever.

Contents

Acknowledgements	6
Foreword	7
Introduction	13

Breakfast & Brunch

The Milestone, London, England	16
Bea's Eggs Royale	17
GoldenEye Resort, Oracabessa Bay, Jamaica	18
Stamp & Go	19
Inn at 202 Dover, Talbot County, Maryland, USA	20
German Apple Pancake	21
Viceroy Bali, Ubud, Bali	22
Salmon Scrambled Eggs	23

Appetizers, Soups & Salads

The Chesterfield Palm Beach, Florida USA	26
Prawn and Lobster Cocktail	27
'41, London, England	28
Cheese Straws and Spiced Nuts	29
The Rubens at the Palace, London, England	30
Chicken Liver Pâté	31
The Egerton House Hotel, London, England	32
Bea's Chicken Soup	33
Blantyre, Lenox, Massachusetts, USA	34
Celeriac Soup	35

Ranch at Rock Creek, Philipsburg, Montana USA   36
   Creek Beet Salad   37

Acorn Inn, Dorset, England   38
   BT's Cabbage Salad   39

Lodge at Kauri Cliffs, Matauri Bay, New Zealand   40
   Kikorangi Blue Cheese, Pear & Vanilla Salad   **41**

MEATS

Dromoland Castle, County Clare, Ireland   44
   Dromoland Irish Stew   45

The Montague on the Gardens, London, England   46
   Lamb in Puff Pastry   47

Hotel d'Angleterre, Geneva, Switzerland   48
   Hand Chopped Sirloin   49

Summer Lodge Country House, Dorset, England   50
   Roast Loin of Dorset Lamb   51

Ranch at Rock Creek, Philipsburg, Montana USA   54
   Braised Leg of Lamb   55

POULTRY

GoldenEye, Jamaica, Caribbean   58
   Jerk Chicken   59

Summer Lodge Country House   60
   Duck Cottage Pie   61

The Oyster Box, Kwa-Zulu Natal, South Africa   62
   Arthur's Chicken Curry   63

Bushmans Kloof, Western Cape, South Africa   64
   Sesame Fried Chicken   65

Hôtel Le Toiny, St Barth, Caribbean   66
   Duckling Filet   67

Ballyfin, County Laois, Ireland — 68
    Organic Chicken with Pearl Barley — 69

Fish

Four Seasons Resort Maui at Wailea, Maui, Hawaii — 72
    Poached Ahi with Apple Fennel Salad — 73

Viceroy Bali, Ubud, Bali — 74
    Lobster Palm Heart with Papaya Coulis — 75

Regent Berlin, Berlin, Germany — 76
    Wild Sea Bass with Grilled Vegetables and Foamed Lobster Sauce — 77

Dromoland, County Clare, Ireland — 78
    Roast Monk Fish, Potatoes and Peas — 79

The Duke of Richmond Hotel, Guernsey, England — 80
    Prawn Stroganoff — 81

Palazzo Avino Ravello, Amalfi Coast, Italy — 82
    King Lobster — 83

The Chesterfield Mayfair, London, England — 84
    Dover Sole — 85

Terre Blanche, Provence, France — 86
    Glazed Turbot with Glazed Peas 'André Moreau' — 87

Pasta

Viceroy Bali, Ubud, Bali — 90
    Vegetarian Cannelloni with Frisée Salad — 91

The Old Government House Hotel and Spa, Guernsey, England — 92
    Pasta Primavera — 93

The Montague on the Gardens, London, England — 94
    Tuna Spaghetti — 95

Desserts

Ashford Castle, County Mayo, Ireland	*98*
Rice Pudding	*99*
Hotel Lungarno, Florence, Italy	*100*
Parfait Vanilla Mousse with Cantaloupe	*101*
Dromoland Castle, County Clare, Ireland	*102*
Crème Caramel with Mango	*103*
The Chesterfield Mayfair, London, England	*104*
Honeycomb Ice Cream	*105*
Ballyfin, County Laois, Ireland	*106*
Summer Strawberry Crumble	*107*
The Twelve Apostles Hotel and Spa, Cape Town, South Africa	*108*
Bea's Cheesecake	*109*
Four Seasons Resort Maui, Maui, Hawaii	*110*
Pickled Mango Sundae	*111*

Recipe Basics   *113*

Metric Measurement Conversions   *121*

Index – by Recipe   *125*

Index – by Hotel/Resort   *128*

About the Author   *131*

INTRODUCTION

There are travel books and there are recipe books. This is a combination of both.

In this first volume of our Taste of Travel series, we are pleased to present a sampling of some of the world's finest hotels and resorts and share with you a little about each of them as well as present its recipe. Some hotels have provided more than one dish in which case we tell you a little more about the property rather than repeat what we revealed earlier. Websites and phone numbers are also included for those of you who want further information about the properties, their restaurants, services and activities.

The recipes range from easy to complex, from breakfast to dessert. Each was provided by the chef who created it, so we do not take credit for any of the culinary creativity.

In Recipe Basics, you'll find tips, definitions and additional recipes you may need to complete some of the main recipes such as the differences between phyllo and puff pastry and instructions for making your own chicken or lamb stock.

If you prefer recipe ingredients in metric measurements, you will also find a Metric Measurement Conversions chapter which provides charts as well as links to online calculators for converting the U.S. measurements to their metric equivalents.

We have also integrated additional photos of favorite scenes from around the world to add to your reading pleasure and remind us of the beauty that surrounds us all.

Enjoy the journey,

LINDA LANG

BREAKFAST & BRUNCH

LONDON, ENGLAND | THE MILESTONE HOTEL
CHENESTON'S RESTAURANT
Chef Kim Sjobakk

Consistently rated as one of London's most exceptional five-star luxury boutique hotels, The Milestone is a magnificent 19th-century architectural treasure centrally located in the Royal Borough of Kensington and Chelsea.

The hotel's award-winning style, warmth and comfort match the excellence of its service. Each of the well-appointed guest rooms, suites and apartments is a work of art adorned with fine fabrics, fresh flowers, antique furnishings and rare artworks.

No two rooms or suites are alike, yet all uphold The Milestone's commitment to extravagance. Some are richly decorated for an intimate, inward-looking mood while others boast stunning views over Kensington Palace and Gardens.

Enjoy modern British cuisine and fine wines in Cheneston's restaurant, afternoon tea beside the Park Lounge's open fire, and signature cocktails in the cozy Stables Bar or chic Conservatory.

The Milestone also has a heated resistance pool, gym, sauna, and chauffeur-driven Bentley if you wish to explore the renowned city sights. The hotel is also within walking distance of the Royal Albert Hall, the exclusive shops of Knightsbridge and close to London's top museums. The West End—London's vibrant, avant-garde theatre district—is just a five-minute taxi ride.

www.milestonehotel.com | Tel: +44 (0) 207 917 1000

Bea's Eggs Royale

Preparation: 20 minutes | Cooking Time: 5 minutes | Serves: 1

Ingredients:

3 eggs
2 oz double cream
1 rounded tbsp butter
1-1/2 tbsp potted shrimp
1 oz smoked salmon,
   cut in strips
2 tsp caviar
2 slices brown bread
rock salt

Method:

- Carefully slice off the tops of the eggs with sharp scissors or a serrated knife.
- Pour eggs into a bowl, whisk and add cream.
- In a sauté pan, melt the butter and then add the egg mixture. Whisk continually until lightly scrambled, achieving the consistency of small curdle cottage cheese.
- Turn off heat to be sure eggs don't overcook and dry out. Season to taste with salt (more will be added with the smoked salmon topping).
- Carefully clean the egg shells. Pour rock salt into three piles on the plate. Place egg shells on the rock salt, pressing lightly, so they stand up.
- Carefully spoon scrambled eggs into shells.
- Top the first egg with a dollop of caviar; the second with the smoked salmon strips; and potted shrimps atop the third.
- Toast the bread and cut each slice into three portions. Serve immediately with the Eggs Royale.

Chef's Tip: Use a rubber-coated whisk to ensure best consistency.

Oracabessa Bay, Jamaica | GoldenEye
Fleming Villa
Chef Talcie Neal

On the north shore of Jamaica just 20 minutes from Ocho Rios is the house that Ian Fleming built. During World War II, he was sent by Naval Intelligence to Jamaica to investigate U-Boat activities in the Caribbean and fell in love with the island. After the war, he chose to remain in his paradise and bought a property on Oracabessa Bay. There he built his dream house—the villa in which he penned the series of James Bond novels.

GoldenEye, named after the code handle for his intelligence mission, now sits on 52 acres. Fleming's historic villa which sleeps 10 is surrounded by two-bedroom villas and lagoon cottages. All are air conditioned with every amenity. The two restaurants, bistro, fine dining, two pools, beach bars, and private beaches nestled in cozy coves offer a paradise of exquisite beauty and pleasure.

In 1976, GoldenEye was purchased by Chris Blackwell, who founded Island Records in 1959 and brought reggae music to the outside world with artists including Bob Marley and the Wailers, and introduced British acts like Traffic, U2, The Chieftains, Bad Company, ELP, Free, King Crimson and more. He added more property to the original 19-acre estate bringing it to the 52-acre resort guests enjoy today.

We suggest you fly into Montego Bay airport as the drive to GoldenEye is faster and more scenic. The resort will, of course, arrange for a driver to meet you at your arrival flight.

www.goldeneye.com | Tel: 1 800 OUTPOST

Stamp & Go

Preparation: 15 minutes | Cooking Time: 15 -20 minutes | Serves: 2

Ingredients:

1/2 lb salt cod cut into 4 pieces
1 small onion
2 long green onions
Scotch bonnet (fresh hot red pepper) to taste
1/2 cup all purpose flour
1 tsp baking powder
1 large tomato
2 cups oil
1 tsp mustard
2 tbsp honey, room temperature

Method:

- Boil salt cod. When almost done, drain and set aside.
- Heat oil in a frying pan.
- Chop onion, spring onions and Scotch bonnet or pepper and mix well.
- Combine flour and baking powder.
- Coat fish well with onion mixture and dip into flour.
- Fry coated fish in hot oil for 5 minutes, turning once.
- Cut tomato into four slices and brown in a grill pan lightly sprayed with oil to prevent burning.
- Drain fish well and serve with a slice of grilled tomato and honey mustard dip.

Honey Mustard Dip:

Mix mustard and honey, then whisk to blend well. Put in a small bowl to serve with fish.

Talbot County, Maryland | Inn at 202 Dover

Peacock Restaurant & Lounge
Chef/Proprietor Ron Mitchell

On the Eastern shore of Chesapeake Bay about 60 miles from Baltimore, historic Talbot County offers a wide variety of recreational activities, cultural events, creative cuisine and delightful small towns.

The Inn at 202 Dover in Easton, owned by Shelby and Ron Mitchell, has earned Four Diamonds from AAA, been named one of the "Top Ten Romantic Inns in America" by *Destinations Travel Magazine* and earned praises from *Food and Wine*, *Travel + Leisure* and American Express. This proud Maryland Historic Inn is also a member of the Historic Hotels of America.

Built in 1874, the beautifully-restored mansion offers five guest accommodations furnished with a charming blend of antiques and reproductions, fine fabrics and linens, European pillow-top mattresses, and all the modern amenities.

In addition to providing bed and breakfast, the inn's Peacock Restaurant & Lounge is Easton's newest culinary hotspot with a menu representing the best of what the county has to offer in classical and contemporary American cuisine.

www.innat202dover.com | Tel: 1 866 450 7600

My Mother's German Apple Pancake

Preparation: 15 minutes | Cooking Time: 25 minutes | Serves: 8

Ingredients:

2 medium Granny Smith apples
1/2 cup butter
4 tbsp granulated sugar
2 tsp cinnamon
2 tsp nutmeg
2 cups Bisquick*
1 cup half & half
2 eggs
4 tbsp powdered sugar

Method:

- Start oven at 375 F.
- Very thinly slice apples with skin on.
- In an 8-inch cast iron skillet, melt butter over a low flame.
- When butter is melted, add sugar, cinnamon and nutmeg and combine completely.
- Slowly add sliced apples, covering the entire bottom of the skillet, and slowly sauté for 3 to 5 minutes.
- Thoroughly mix the eggs and half and half.
- Sift the Bisquick and then add the egg mixture. Mix thoroughly.
- Make sure that the batter is easy to pour but not watery. If necessary, add a bit more half and half. Not too much though.
- Slowly pour the batter into the skillet making sure that you cover all the apples.
- Keep on top of the stove over a low flame for about 10 minutes.
- Carefully lift the skillet with either a glove or towel and place it in the oven, top shelf.
- After about 15 minutes, check with a toothpick to ensure that it is done. Then, bake for another three to four minutes.
- Remove the skillet and place a plate over the top and carefully turn the skillet over. The pancake should come right out on to the plate.
- Allow the pancake three to five minutes to rest.
- Slice into 8 servings and then sprinkle powdered sugar on each slice.
- Some folks like to have syrup with the pancake. Ensure that it is warm.

See Recipe Basics for substitution

Ubud, Bali | Viceroy Bali
CasCades Restaurant
Chef Nic Vanderbeeken

High on a secluded ridge overlooking the Valley of the Kings is Viceroy Bali, a luxurious 25-villa hideaway for those seeking the exclusive, the exotic, the elegant.

Once a retreat for the royals, the resort offers marvelous views of the valley below. The villas, each with its own pool and exquisite Balinese décor, provide every amenity and the ultimate setting for renewal, relaxation and tranquility.

Activities include the luxurious Lembah Spa and Beauty Centre, complete gym, wellness center, onsite helipad and soon—a tennis facility and yoga pavilion.

The award-winning restaurant, CasCades, overseen by Chef Nic Vanderbeeken, has been ranked one of Indonesia's top five restaurants by *The Miele Guide 2011/2012*. The guide, which identifies Asia's top 20 dining spots, is based on a jury of restaurateurs, food critics and writers, and a popular vote.

Guests also have access to the infinity pool, boutique, and library.

A member of Small Luxury Hotels, Viceroy Bali is located within minutes from Ubud, one of Southeast Asia's most delightful villages with its focus on culture, yoga and nature and quaint shops, galleries and cafes.

www.viceroybali.com | Tel: +62 361 971 777

Salmon Scrambled Eggs

Preparation: 10 minutes | Cooking Time: 5 minutes | Serves: 1

Ingredients:

2 thin slices of smoked salmon
2 tsp fresh chopped Italian parsley
1 tsp pickled ginger*
2 eggs
1 tbsp cream (before cooking)
1 tbsp cream (after cooking)
1 tsp butter
1 tsp canola
1 qt of oil for deep frying
salt and pepper to taste
1 phyllo cup*

Method:

- Cut salmon into very thin slices and mix with parsley.
- Deep fry the pickled ginger. Strain carefully and cut into chunky pieces.
- Whisk eggs and mix with 1 tbsp cream.
- Melt butter and 1 tbsp oil in a pan. Add egg mixture and stir continually until almost done.
- Remove from heat and stir in second tbsp of cream. Add salt and pepper to taste.
- Add salmon and ginger to egg mixture, stirring until done to taste.
- Top with a curled slice of smoked salmon and sprinkling of parsley.
- Spoon into phyllo cup and top with a curl of salmon and sprinkle of parsley leaves..

See Recipe Basics

FIVE STAR RECIPES FROM WORLD FAMOUS HOTELS & RESORTS

VENICE

APPETIZERS, SOUPS & SALADS

Palm Beach, Florida | Chesterfield Palm Beach
Leopard Lounge & Restaurant
Executive Chef Gerard Couglin

The four-star Chesterfield Palm Beach is an elegant boutique hotel encapsulating the luxurious, casual Palm Beach lifestyle. This historic landmark, which sits on an exclusive resort island, is well known for its exquisite European style and world-class service.

By day, the hotel is a sunny oasis where guests relax around the pool. With the evening comes live entertainment, dancing, and gourmet dining at the highly-acclaimed Leopard Lounge and Restaurant making it one of the liveliest spots in the area.

Each of the luxurious rooms and suites are individually designed to reflect the colors and atmosphere of Palm Beach's clear, warm days and soft, cool nights. Here you enjoy all the amenities including air-conditioning, cable TV and complimentary Wi-Fi.

The Leopard Restaurant offers an eclectic, imaginative menu matched by an excellent wine selection. The Courtyard, a secret garden haven rich with palms and potted flowers, is perfect for breakfast, lunch, afternoon tea or a romantic dinner. You may also choose to dine on the Terrace, by the pool, or take advantage of 24-hour room service.

The Leopard Lounge is a vibrant social hub, popular with locals and celebrities. The barman's specialties are exotic cocktails, and you can dance the night away to live music.

The Chesterfield Palm Beach is a member of Small Luxury Hotels of the World and is ideally located just two blocks from the exclusive shops of Worth Avenue. Also within easy reach is the West Palm Beach business district, City Place shopping and dining, and the Palm Beach Airport.

www.chesterfieldpb.com | Tel: +1 561 659 5800

Prawn and Lobster Cocktail

Preparation Time: 30 minutes | Cooking Time: 10 minutes | Serves: 4

Ingredients:

2 cups cooked lobster meat or crayfish cut into 3/4 inch chunks
20 medium cooked prawns cut into 3/4 inch chunks (reserve 4 whole prawns for garnish)
1 head iceberg lettuce
2 lemons
salt and pepper

For Marie Rose Sauce:
1/2 cup good quality mayonnaise
1/4 cup sour cream
3/4 cup tomato ketchup
1/2 tsp Worcestershire Sauce
1 tbsp lemon juice
3 drops tobacco sauce*
1 tbsp brandy

Method:

- Whisk all the sauce ingredients together. Add salt and pepper to taste.
- Finely shred lettuce. Use a pretty cocktail glass or porcelain dish and fill up halfway with lettuce.
- Mix the shellfish with enough sauce to coat it well. Place mixture on top of lettuce and spoon a little more sauce on top.
- Garnish with half a lemon and whole prawn hanging over the edge.

or Tabasco Sauce

London, England | '41
Lounge & In-Room Dining

'41 is a discreet, residents-only boutique hotel ideally located in the heart of London just behind Buckingham Palace. Its chic black-and-white interior design is complemented by rich mahogany throughout the hotel, and the glass ceiling of the Executive Lounge floods the room with natural daylight.

Opened in 2001, this intimate property offers the height of five-star luxury. Its beautiful 30 rooms and suites include two unique hospitality suites, butler service, 24-hour room service and the latest in-room technology. The skilled staff outnumbers guests two-to-one, providing full concierge service and an exceptional level of personalized service.

Boasting one of London's prime locations, the hotel overlooks The Royal Mews—a branch of the Lord Chamberlain's Office that provides road transport for The Queen and members of the Royal Family by both horse-drawn carriage and motor car. Ideally situated for business or leisure, the hotel is only five minutes from Victoria Station.

'41 offers a unique boutique hotel experience with 24-hour informal and personalized dining. You can enjoy sunlit breakfasts in the Executive Lounge, appreciate the stunning view from the Mezzanine level, or savor the ultimate in-room dining experience. An unusual feature is the hotel's invitation to "Plunder the Pantry," where guests are free to graze on delicious complimentary snacks throughout the day and night.

Next door is bbar, a popular lounge and dining spot which, under the same ownership at the hotel, offers excellent casual dining.

www.41hotel.com | Tel: +44 (0) 20 7300 0041

Cheese Straws and Spiced Nuts

Preparation Time: 30 minutes | Cooking Time: 1.5 hours | Serves: 8

Ingredients:

Cheese Straws:
1 sheet store-bought puff pastry
1 cup strong cheddar cheese, finely grated
1/4 cup parmesan, finely grated
pinch of cayenne or paprika
pinch of salt and pepper

Spiced Nuts:
1 egg white
1 lb pecans or walnuts
1/2 cup sugar
2 tsp ground cinnamon
3/4 tsp ground ginger
1 tsp ground coriander
1 tsp salt

Method:

Cheese Straws:
- Carefully unroll pastry and smooth out on a floured board and sprinkle with all the ingredients.
- Lightly roll up pastry to compress the coating, then press and fold the roll lengthwise so that the ends meet.
- With a sharp knife, cut the roll lengthwise into 4-inch wide strips.
- Give each strip a twist and place on a baking sheet covered with parchment paper.
- Place tray in freezer for 20 minutes, then bake in a 350°F oven for 15 minutes until golden brown.
- Cool on a baking rack before serving.

Spiced Nuts:
- Whisk egg white with a tbsp of water until foamy, then coat nuts with the mixture.
- Mix sugar and spices in a bowl then stir in the coated nuts. Bake at 260°F for 15 minutes, then reduce temperature to 210°F and bake until crunchy.

LONDON, ENGLAND | THE RUBENS AT THE PALACE

THE LIBRARY RESTAURANT
Executive Chef Nelson Linhares

The Rubens is located in the heart of London overlooking the Royal Mews of Buckingham Palace. First opening as a hotel in 1912, it hosted debutantes and high-society guests of Buckingham Palace. Today, the magnificent building retains its original historical splendor, and it is rated as one of the highest four-star London hotels.

The Palace Lounge and Cavalry Bar are extremely popular among guests and locals alike. The Old Master's Restaurant offers succulent roasts, while the Library Restaurant serves scrumptious award-winning English cuisine. At the end of the day, relax and unwind in the safari-chic surroundings of the Leopard Champagne Bar or the trendy bbar.

The Rubens at the Palace offers 143 deluxe guest rooms, eight royal rooms, 10 luxurious suites, and a private royal wing of superior rooms with a British Monarchy theme. All rooms and suites are lavishly furnished and guests may choose from a selection of elegant rooms overlooking the Royal Mews.

A favorite spot for afternoon tea is the magnificent Palace Lounge, a bright open space with panoramic views of The Royal Mews and the Queen's stables. There is a Pet Concierge as well as a dedicated Children's Concierge with a "Director of Fun" to assist families visiting London. The Rubens is close to the most popular attractions, the majestic Royal Parks, shops, theatres, museums and is also very near Victoria Station.

www.rubenshotel.com | Tel: +44 (0) 20 7834 6600

Chicken Liver Pâté

Preparation time: 30 | Cooking time: 20 minutes | Serves: 6-8

Ingredients:

9 oz chicken liver
chicken stock or water
   (enough to cover livers)
3-1/2 oz softened butter
1 tsp salt
pinch of Cayenne pepper
1/2 tsp nutmeg
1 tsp dry mustard
1/8 tsp ground cloves
2 tbsp onion, very finely minced
1 tbsp brandy
clarified butter for sealing*
truffles (optional)
few slices whole wheat bread
   and/or a baguette

Method:

- In a saucepan, cover the chicken livers with chicken stock (or water) and bring to a boil. Cover and simmer for 15-20 minutes.
- Drain the livers and put them through the finest blade of a food chopper, then mix thoroughly with the remaining ingredients.
- Blend well before packing the mixture into ramekins. Top or seal each ramekin with the clarified butter and chill in refrigerator.
- Serve on a small silver tray or decorative plate with cornichons and thin, toasted slices of whole wheat bread and/or baguettes.

See Recipe Basics

London, England | The Egerton House Hotel
Custom Dining-In Fare

The Egerton House Hotel is a charming, luxurious five-star townhouse located in the heart of fashionable Knightsbridge. Quietly tucked away on a tree-lined street in one of London's most prestigious districts, the city's finest museums and shops are within walking distance and Kensington Gardens and Hyde Park are just to the north.

This lovely boutique property embodies comfort, hospitality, and is renowned for its personalized service. Throughout the hotel, lavish fabrics and furnishings are complemented by original works of art and fine antiques. The beautiful dining room is ideal for private functions, and its cozy lounge serves a fine English afternoon tea.

With views of Egerton Gardens and the Victoria & Albert Museum, you can see much of Knightsbridge from the upper floor windows. Buckingham Palace is a mile to the east and the West End is also nearby. To the south, you'll find the Royal Hospital Chelsea, where the Chelsea Flower Show--Britain's leading horticultural event--is held each May. Pets are also welcomed like royalty at the Egerton. The hotel staff goes out of its way to make sure your four-legged family member receives first-class hospitality. The Pet Concierge service includes food and water bowls, a turndown pet treat, toys and treats, special dining menus and they can arrange a trip to the Pet Spa at Harrods.

www.redcarnationhotels.com/egertonhousehotel | Tel: +44 (0) 20 7589 2412

Bea's Chicken Soup

Preparation Time: 1 hour | Cooking Time: 1 hour | Serves: 8

Ingredients:

- 3 2-1/4 lb chickens, quartered with gizzards, neck and feet, if possible
- 4 large whole carrots
- 4 stalks celery
- 2 medium onions, whole
- 4 large leeks, cut in half
- 3 bay leaves
- 8 peppercorns
- 2-3 organic chicken bouillon cubes (in lieu of salt)
- 6 sprigs parsley
- 1/4 lb fine noodles, cooked separately

Method:

- Put chicken, carrots, celery, onions, leeks, bay leaf, peppercorns and parsley in a large sauce pan and cover with water.
- Bring to a boil and add two chicken bouillon cubes and skim.
- Simmer for about six hours, then strain mixture into a clean sauce pan.
- Dice a handful of chicken meat and carrots from the soup into 1/3-inch cubes and set aside.
- Bring soup back to a boil and test for seasoning. Add another bouillon cube if needed.
- To serve, spoon into individual soup bowls, adding a few cooked noodles, diced chicken and carrots to each serving.

Bea's Tip: This recipe is also excellent for making a strong chicken stock.

Lenox, Massachusettes | Blantyre
Blantyre Dining Room
Chef Arnaud Cotar

Built in 1902 and fashioned after an ancestral home in Scotland, Blantyre immediately transports you into a gentle by-gone era as you approach the romantic ivy-covered main house at the end of the wooded drive.

This privately owned country-house hotel in the Berkshire Hills is surrounded by theatres, dance and music festivals in summer and is a winter wonderland when the weather turns cold. Overstuffed chairs, fresh flowers and treasures galore fill rooms with leaded-glass windows looking out onto sweeping lawns and historic trees.

In all, this Forbes Five Star hotel is home to 21 luxurious accommodations, each individually furnished with period pieces and treasured heirlooms. Blantyre has also been a member of the prestigious Relais et Châteaux since 1983.

After a day of hiking, ice skating or snowshoeing on Blantyre's 117 acres, you can lounge in the intimate Potting Shed Spa where total relaxation awaits. In summer, relax by the heated outdoor swimming pool with an ice cream and good mystery or a book of poetry from Blantyre's collection of 4000+ volumes.

The changing dinner menu reflects the best of each season, and the candlelit dining room ambience is completed by the soft musical strains of a nearby pianist. The award-winning wine cellar houses 12,000 bottles from which to choose the perfect accompaniment to your dinner. For family gatherings, weddings or corporate events, the property is available for exclusive takeovers.

From the Snow Concierge helping with winter boots to the Sommelier pairing a fine wine with Chef Arnaud Cotar's imaginative French-American cuisine, the staff of 70 pampers you with every care and attention.

www.blantyre.com | Tel: 1 413 637 3556

Celeriac Soup

Preparation Time: 40 minutes | Cooking Time: 45 minutes | Serves: 8

Ingredients:

1 celeriac (about 1-3/4 to 2 lbs)
1 leek, white and pale green part only, washed and sliced
1 10-inch celery stalk, diced
1 small clove garlic, chopped
1 medium onion, peeled and diced
1 bay leaf
6 cups water
1 tsp salt or to taste
1 cup light cream

Method:

- Peel the celeriac and cut it into 1-inch cubes. You should have about 5 cups.
- Put cubes into a soup pan along with the leek, celery, garlic, onion, bay leaf, water and salt to taste. Bring to a boil and then simmer the vegetables for about 20-25 minutes or until they are all very tender.
- Strain the mixture, reserving the liquid.
- Purée the vegetables in a food processor or through a food mill.
- Return to the pan, add the reserved liquid and bring to simmering again. Stir in the cream and then check for seasoning, adding more salt if you prefer it.

Optional:

In the center of the bowl of soup, you may add a juicy seared scallop or a scoop of lobster or crab salad which has been bound with a touch of mayonnaise.

Chef's Tip: The soup can be made a day ahead, chilled, then re-warmed over low heat and whisked to re-combine the ingredients.

Philipsburg, Montana | Ranch at Rock Creek
Granite Lodge
Executive Chef Josh Drage

Granite County was discovered during the silver mining boom of the late 1800s when Philipsburg's Hope Mill became the first silver mill in Montana. Nearby Granite Mill, the state's greatest silver producer, was home to some 3,000 residents until the Silver Crash of 1893 devastated the mining business. At the same time, Utah cattle baron Fred Burr brought cattle ranching to the Flint Creek Valley, a business that has continued through the decades.

Originally a mining claim in the late 1800s, the Ranch at Rock Creek was homesteaded as a cattle ranch which is still operated today by current owner Jim Manley who purchased the property in 2007 after his lifelong search for the perfect ranch.

Today, ranch life at the Ranch at Rock Creek combines all the modern luxuries with the best of authentic ranch living and rich variety of outdoor experiences. The Granite Lodge serves as the activity hub. Here you'll find the Great room, dining room, Silver Dollar Saloon, an outdoor pool with patio and Jacuzzi, the Granite Spa and the Mercantile. Chef Drage's world-class cuisine is seasonally influenced and features Montana-raised beef, lamb, chicken and dairy products along with local, organically grown produce.

www.theranchatrockcreek.com | Tel: 1 877 377 8056

FIVE STAR RECIPES FROM WORLD FAMOUS HOTELS & RESORTS

Creek Beet Salad

Preparation Time: 45 minutes | Cooking Time: 1 hour | Serves: 4-6

Ingredients:

6 medium-large beets
1 lemon
1 orange
3 twigs of thyme
olive oil
sea salt
1 bunch of cress
1 small bunch of parsley
1 kumquat
Marcona almonds to taste
1/2 cup chevre (goat cheese)
1 cup olive oil
fresh mint
1/2 cup white balsamic
salt and pepper

Method:

Roast Beets:
- Trim and clean the ends of the beets. Place beets on a long piece of aluminum foil centering it on one side so the foil is able to be folded back on itself to be sealed.
- Halve the orange and lemon and place on the beets along with a bit of olive oil and fresh thyme.
- Fold the foil over on itself and seal the edges by crimping tight. Roast in a 400ºF oven for an hour, the foil will puff up with air making a pillow shape.
- Remove from oven and let rest for a half hour without puncturing the foil.

Vinaigrette:
- In a blender, add the goat cheese, mint, white balsamic, salt and pepper. Turn blender on and drizzle the oil through the top of the blender until fully incorporated.

To Serve:
- Remove beets from the foil and again trim the tops and bottoms. Peel off skin with a paring knife. Quarter the beets and set aside.
- Trim off the cress leaves. Slice the kumquat, removing any seeds. Pick the parsley. On the plate, place a small puddle of the vinaigrette, and build the salad on the vinaigrette, garnishing with the almonds, white anchovy and parsley.

Dorset, England | Acorn Inn
The Pub

The Acorn Inn is a wonderful blend of traditional village pub life, good company and an award-winning restaurant. Built in the 16th century of local honey-colored stone, this old coaching inn retains its original historical character and charm. Thomas Hardy refers to it as "The Sow & Acorn" in *Tess of the d'Urbervilles*.

Today, the décor of old beams, low ceilings, oak paneling and flagstone floors is elegantly maintained.

The 10 comfortable en-suite hotel rooms in the family and pet-friendly inn are named after places in Hardy's novels and provide the most modern creature comforts complemented with traditional fabrics and furnishings.

The country pub is very much in the heart of the community with its lively bar frequented by regulars who enjoy the ales, quiz nights and skittles leagues. The restaurant also wins top accolades from the serious foodies who return regularly for the exceptional gastro experience.

If you feel the need for a spa treatment, stroll across the road to the Inn's sister property, Summer Lodge, and enjoy some pampering in their spa. There's also a gorgeous indoor pool, sauna, gym and Jacuzzi as well as treatment rooms. Should you wish to explore the countryside by bike, horseback or other means, the Inn can assist with those arrangements.

http://acorn-inn.co.uk | Tel: +44 (0) 1935 83228

BT's Cabbage Salad

Preparation Time: 30 minutes | Cooking Time: (none) | Serves: 4-6

Ingredients:

1 1 lb firm head of cabbage
1 3-1/2 oz bunch of green onions
6 stalks celery
juice of 2 lemons
7 oz canola or vegetable oil
4 tbsp sugar
2 minced cloves garlic

Method:

- Select a cabbage with lots of outer dark leaves. Cut into pieces about 3/4-inch square.
- Chop the spring onion and celery into 1/2-inch square pieces. Toss cabbage, celery, onion and garlic together in a serving bowl.
- Mix the sugar, lemon juice and oil and pour over cabbage mixture. Season to taste with salt and pepper and toss well to combine.

Chef's Tip: Salad will stay fresh in fridge for up to one week.

MATAURI BAY, NEW ZEALAND | LODGE AT KAURI CLIFFS

Main Lodge Dining Room
Executive Chef Barry Frith

One of the most awarded luxury boutique golf & spa resort hotels in New Zealand, the Lodge at Kauri Cliffs sits on 6,000 acres near Matauri Bay. The main lodge features spectacular 180-degree views of the Pacific Ocean, Cape Brett and the Cavalli Islands that can be viewed from the verandas, lounge, card and dining rooms.

The Lodge accommodates 22 guest suites or you can opt for one of the 11 guest cottages neighboring the native bush which look across the golf course and Pacific. Each suite offers its own private veranda, bedroom with sitting area and open fireplace, walk-in his and hers wardrobes and a bathroom with a shower, tub and his and hers vanities.

Facilities include two Astroturf tennis courts, infinity swimming pool with spa, and fully equipped fitness centre. There are also three secluded swimming beaches and several waterfalls which provide wonderful settings for picnics and barbecues. Breakfast, lunch and dinner may be enjoyed on the veranda as well as in the main dining room. The dinner menu changes nightly and features the finest local meats, fish and produce. And you'll want to save room for the pastry chef's exotic temptations. To work off any extra calories, head for the spa or gym.

The par 72 championship Kauri Cliffs golf course, designed and built by David Harman of Golf Course Consultants, Orlando, Florida, offers five sets of tees to challenge every skill level. Fifteen holes view the Pacific Ocean, six of which are played alongside cliffs that plunge to the sea. The beautiful inland holes wind through marsh, forest and farmland.

In addition to activities on the property, nearby options include world famous game fishing, scuba diving, snorkeling, sailing, sea kayaking, horseback riding, nature walks, hunting for boar and more. There are several ways to discover the unspoiled scenic splendors of Northland and the Bay of Islands which are home to some 144 isles, secluded bays and coves with vibrant histories and colorful marine life.

www.kauricliffs.com | Tel: +64 9 407 0010 or in North America only: 1 949 487 0522

Kikorangi Blue Cheese, Pear & Vanilla Salad

Preparation Time: 1-2 hours | Cooking Time: 30 minutes | Serves: 4

Ingredients:

Poached Pears & Purée:
2 Anjou pears
8 oz water
4 oz white wine
4 oz chardonnay vinegar
1 cup sugar
2 star anise
1 cinnamon stick
2 pieces orange peel
1 shallot slice
1 clove garlic
1/4 scraped vanilla pod
dash of pear liqueur

Vinaigrette:
4 oz hazelnut oil
4 tsp chardonnay vinegar
1 heaping tsp Dijon mustard
pinch of salt and pepper
pinch vanilla seeds

For Serving:
1 pear with skin on, thinly sliced lengthwise
1 small handful of greens such as arugula, kale, or mustard leaves, torn in small pieces

Method:

- For white wine pears: Peel and core the pears and discard the peelings and core.
- In a medium sauce pan, mix the remaining ingredients and bring to a boil.
- Poach the pears whole in the mixture for 15-20 minutes. Remove pan from stove and let mixture cool. When cool, take out pears and cut into presentable pieces (cubes or rectangles) and set aside.
- For the purée: place the remaining pear pieces in a blender with the scraped vanilla pod and a dash of pear liquor. Blend until smooth.
- For the red wine pears: use same ingredients as for white pears, but replace the white wine with red wine and the chardonnay vinegar with cabernet sauvignon vinegar, and cook the same way. No need to purée.
- For best results, cook the pears a day ahead for great taste and color.

Vinaigrette:
- Mix first four ingredients together well, then add a small amount of vanilla seeds. Mix again.

To Serve:
- Smear purée in the center of the plate, top with red and white pears cubes and sprinkle tops with bits of chopped salad greens.
- Put the raw pear slices in a bowl and dress with the vinaigrette. Then roll up the pear slices into little tubes and garnish the plate.
- Drizzle some vinaigrette over and around the ingredients and garnish with a fresh herb or baby leaf.

Chef's Tip: *For extra crunch, serve some candied nuts.*

Bora Bora

MEATS

County Clare, Ireland | Dromoland Castle

The Earl of Thurmond
Executive Chef David McCann

One of the most famous baronial castles in Ireland, Dromoland was once the ancestral home of the O'Briens, the Barons of Inchiquin- one of the few native Gaelic families of royal blood and direct descendants of Brian Boroimhe (Boru, High King of Ireland in the 11 century.)

Built of dark blue limestone and surrounded by some 1,500 acres of estate grounds, feral lakes and woodlands home to red deer, pheasant, partridge and many fauna, Dromoland Castle offers the perfect setting for a relaxing getaway far removed from daily challenges or a vacation for the entire family.

The quadrangle of 28 guest rooms, built in 1736 by Sir Edward O'Brien, is almost a century older than the rest of the five-star hotels in Ireland. Luxurious accommodations feature cottage-style décor based on 18th Century botanical drawings complemented by sumptuous upholstery designed by the French Fabric House Pierre Frey. Modern amenities include Interactive TV with music and movies-on-demand and broadband Internet access, and American socket converters. You also receive Dromoland Castle's signature slippers and bathrobes. If you're traveling with the family, the kids are offered specially tailored children's menus, selection of board games, and children's TV channels and movies on request.

Dining at Dromoland ranges from fine dining in the award-winning Earl of Thomond to casual fare in the Fig Tree restaurant and light snacks at the country club. You can also have a picnic that includes a bottle of champagne. The cocktail bar, with spectacular views of the county's lakes, is also a popular gathering spot.

Also available for your pleasure is a beautiful spa, a wealth of activities including horseback riding, fishing, archery, falconry, clay shooting, tennis, walking tours, and for golfers a championship course designed by Irish golfing legend J.B. Carr and one of golf's finest course architects, Ron Kirby.

www.dromoland.ie | Tel: +353 61 368144

Dromoland Irish Stew

Preparation Time: 1 hour | Cooking Time: 2 hours | Serves: 4

Ingredients:

2-1/4 lbs neck and shoulder lamb, cubed
2 onions, diced
4 tbsp pearl barley, soaked in water 1 hour
3 carrots, peeled and sliced
3 sticks celery, washed and sliced
2 leeks, washed and sliced
3 potatoes, peeled
2 tsp chopped parsley
1 spring thyme
1 bay leaf
1 quart white lamb stock *

Method:

- Soak cubed lamb in cold water overnight in fridge. Wash thoroughly under running water before cooking.
- Place lamb in a large pot, cover with cold water and bring to a boil. Discard water.
- Place the meat back in the pot and cover with lamb stock. Bring to a boil and skim. Add the onion thyme, bay leaf, and season lightly with salt and freshly ground pepper. Simmer about 1-1/2 hours or until cooked.
- Add the drained soaked barley half way through the cooking time of the meat.
- While meat is cooking, boil the potatoes, drain well, mash and keep warm.
- Separately cook all the vegetables until tender and refresh in iced water. Drain and set aside.
- To finish, remove the lamb from the stock and cover with cling film.
- Thicken the stock with mashed potatoes. Return lamb along with the cooked vegetables, bring to a boil for 2 minutes, check the seasoning, and finish with chopped parsley.
- Serve with Worcestershire Sauce and Tabasco Sauce.

Chef's Tip: Don't cut the lamb too small. If it is not soaked properly, the broth will have a dull grey color.

See Recipe Basics

London, England | The Montague on the Gardens

The Blue Door Bistro
Executive Chef Martin Halls

The Montague on the Gardens is an elegant, long-established Georgian townhouse overlooking a secluded private garden square in the heart of one of central London's most attractive and fashionable areas. This beautiful four-star boutique hotel provides excellent personal service, understated comfort and outstanding value. Despite being in the heart of the city, you feel like you are secluded in a comfortable country home. The 88 exquisitely-appointed rooms, 11 suites, and one apartment suite are gracefully understated, furnished with exquisite fabrics capturing the hotel's literary heritage and the timeless elegance of Bloomsbury with its charming garden squares. All rooms include independent air-conditioning, complimentary Internet and Wi-Fi.

The Montague boasts a wide range of dining options. The Blue Door Bistro specializes in modern European cuisine, and its dishes may also be enjoyed al fresco on the delightful terrace overlooking the idyllic private gardens of the Bedford Estate. You can also savor the hotel's legendary afternoon tea in the Conservatory, enjoy a Cuban on the Cigar Terrace, or relax in the cozy Terrace Bar.

The hotel is within strolling distance of the West End and British Museum, and a mere five minutes from the Eurostar terminal at St. Pancras. You are also just minutes from London's Financial District, Covent Garden, shopping on Oxford and Bond Streets, the West End theatres and Russell and Bloomsbury Squares.

www.montaguehotel.com | Tel: +44 (0) 20 7637 1001

Lamb in Puff Pastry

Preparation Time: 4 hours | Cooking Time: 30-40 minutes | Serves: 6-8

Ingredients:

2-1/4 lbs lean lamb from leg cut into 1-inch cubes
1 large onion, finely chopped
3 carrots, minced
3 celery sticks, minced
1 sprig each fresh rosemary and thyme
1 cup flour seasoned with 1 tbsp salt, 1/2 tbsp pepper, 1/2 tsp ground ginger, and 2 tbsp paprika
1 qt lamb (or vegetable or chicken) stock
vegetable oil
1 package frozen puff pastry dough*
1 egg yolk

Method:

- In a large roasting pan with cover, heat 4 oz of oil. Brown the celery, carrots and onion over a medium heat.
- Remove vegetables and set aside.
- Lightly dust the lamb cubes with seasoned flour. In the same roasting pan, brown on all sides.
- To start creating the sauce, pour in a little stock, then return the vegetables and add the thyme and rosemary and blend.
- Scrape bottom of the pan to loosen any browned bits, stir well, cover and reduce heat to a simmer.
- Cook for an hour or until the lamb is very tender and the sauce has reduced to a thickened consistency. Adjust the seasonings as necessary. Cool to room temperature then refrigerate overnight.
- Form the lamb into a loaf and wrap in puff pastry. Brush with egg yolk and place on a baking sheet with the seam underneath.
- Bake at 390° F for about 30 minutes until nicely browned. Allow to cool for a minute before presenting at the table and slicing into 1 to 1-1/2 inch pieces.

*For best timing, note preparation time on package directions. To make your own puff pastry, see Recipe Basics.

Geneva, Switzerland | Hôtel d'Angleterre

Windows Restaurant
Executive Chef Philippe Audonnet

Dating back to 1872, Hotel d'Angleterre overlooking Lake Geneva is the original work of the famed architect Anthony Krafft and today is acknowledged as one of Geneva's heritage sites. Originally conceived as an exclusive luxury hotel offering just 30 spacious rooms—most with a spectacular view of Lake Geneva and Mont Blanc—the hotel blends old-world charm with new-world service. Majestic views of the surrounding mountains and Jet d'Eau—a large fountain and one of the city's most famous landmarks—provide a spectacular setting for this opulent gem. Its ideal location in the heart of Geneva's shopping and financial districts is also close to the airport, the railway station, and just an hour from superb Alpine skiing.

Hotel d'Angleterre's renowned Windows Restaurant offers breathtaking views of the lake and Mont Blanc with fine cuisine and wines to match. Traditional afternoon teas are a popular institution, while the sophisticated and extremely popular Leopard Room and Bar comes to life in the evenings with contemporary live music and extensive cocktail and wine list. It is widely regarded as one of the best in Geneva and the *Hideaway Guide* named it "Hotel Bar of the Year". The atmosphere is intimate, chic and vibrant with a versatile live band.

The hotel also boasts an extensive fitness center and sauna. The d'Angleterre is a favorite venue for exclusive weddings and honeymoons as well as birthdays, anniversaries, business meetings and banquets.

Consistently voted as one of *TripAdvisor's* top Hotels, this exquisite Leading Hotels of the World member well deserves its long list of accolades.

www.dangleterrehotel.com | Tel: +41 (0) 22 906 5514

HAND CHOPPED SIRLOIN

Preparation Time: 45 minutes | Cooking Time: 6-15 minutes | Serves: 1

Ingredients:

7 oz hand-chopped sirloin
1 tbsp chopped dark golden brown onion
1 tsp melted butter
1 tbsp strong chicken stock made from organic cubes
fresh ground pepper to taste

Method:

- Mix the meat and onions.
- Mix the butter and stock. Gradually add the mixture to the chopped steak and onions so it does not become too mushy to hold together.
- Form into a New York strip shape, about 1 inch thick and let it settle. Smooth slightly, very gently.
- Heat a cast iron skillet until very hot. Grease with a little oil or butter – or use a cast iron non-stick pan with no oil. Add the meat and grill until it makes a firm crust. Turn only once and do not press down on the meat while cooking.
- Serve with a few cherry tomatoes and hand-cut fries.

DORSET, ENGLAND | SUMMER LODGE COUNTRY HOUSE

The Restaurant
Executive Chef Steven Titman

Summer Lodge Country House Hotel, Restaurant and Spa, an exquisite five-star property set deep in Hardy's Wessex, offers the ultimate escape. Hidden in the pretty village of Evershot in the picturesque Dorsetshire countryside, this charming 24 bedroom Relais & Châteaux property ranks among the finest country house hotels in England. Each of the 20 rooms and four luxury suites weaves its own spell with rich fabrics, elegant furnishings and the latest entertainment technology.

Dorset is a delightful blend of thatched villages, literary resonances, geological treasures, and sweeping chalk cliffs. It has it all—narrow winding lanes, ivy-clad cottages, and invigorating countryside—and Wessex, so named by Thomas Hardy and used as a major setting in his novels.

Summer Lodge Executive Chef Steve Titman makes imaginative use of the abundant fresh local produce, creating traditional English dishes with a twist of modern European influences using herbs from the hotel's own kitchen garden. *Wine Spectator* rates the wine list as one of the most outstanding in the world. Traditional afternoon teas are served either on the terrace or in the drawing room designed by Thomas Hardy, himself. The spa is a seductive sanctuary to refresh and rejuvenate, purify and detoxify. Guests can also unwind in a fully-equipped gym, Jacuzzi, sauna and heated indoor pool. Summer Lodge also offers family-friendly accommodations in the Coach House and Summer Lane Cottages.

www.summerlodgehotel.co.uk | Tel: +44 (0)1935 482000

ROAST LOIN OF DORSET LAMB
AND BRAISED SHOULDER SHEPHERD'S PIE WITH SAVOY CABBAGE AND ROSEMARY JUS

Preparation: 45 minutes | Cooking Time: 5-6 hours | Serves: 4

Ingredients:

Roast Loin of Lamb:
2 5-oz lamb loins

Braised Shoulder of Lamb:
1-1/4 lbs lamb shoulder (de-boned and trimmed)
2 onions, 1 chopped and 1 finely diced
2 carrots, 1 chopped and 1 finely diced
3 garlic cloves
1 tbsp tomato purée
3-1/2 oz tomato juice
7 oz red wine
1 pt lamb or chicken stock
1/2 celeriac, finely diced
1 swede (rutabaga or yellow turnip), finely diced

Rosemary Jus:
2 sprigs rosemary finely chopped

Potato Ring:
2 large maris piper (Irish) potatoes. (russets or red skinned potatoes with golden flesh can be substituted.)

Potato Foam:
1-1/4 cup potato purée
1/3 cup milk
3-1/2 oz cream
3-1/2 tbsp butter
salt and freshly milled black pepper

Savoy Cabbage:
6 rashers bacon, cut into lardons*
1/2 onion, finely chopped
1/2 savoy cabbage, shredded

Equipment:

1 Isi cream whipper (with 2 gas cartridges)
4 metal rings - 2 inch diameter
butchers string
mandolin

* 6 strips cut into small pieces

continued...

FIVE STAR RECIPES FROM WORLD FAMOUS HOTELS & RESORTS

Roast Loin of Dorset Lamb
and Braised Shoulder Shepherd's Pie with Savoy Cabbage and Rosemary Jus

Method:

Braised Shoulder Shepherd's Pie:
- Season the lamb shoulder and sear in a hot frying pan. Place the lamb in a deep casserole dish.
- In the same frying pan add the chopped onions, carrots and garlic and cook for 3 minutes.
- Add the tomato purée and cook for a further 2 minutes, then add the tomato juice, red wine and stock. Bring to a boil and pour over the shoulder.
- Cover the dish and place in a slow 285° F oven and braise for 5 to 6 hours or until the shoulder is falling apart. Remove the shoulder. Allow to cool slightly and flake or roughly chop the meat.
- Meanwhile, strain the cooking juice and reduce in a saucepan until well flavored and sauce has a good consistency.
- In a clean saucepan, cook the diced carrot, onion, celeriac and swede until soft (but not puréed). Add the diced shoulder and continue to cook on a low heat. Add a little of the sauce to bind the lamb and vegetables together. Save the rest of the sauce to one side.

Potato Ring:
- Thinly slice the potato lengthwise with a mandolin.
- Wrap a length of greaseproof paper around a metal ring and then carefully arrange the potato slices onto it, securing with a piece of string.
- Deep fry until golden brown. As the potato cooks, the ring and paper should fall away allowing the potato to cook evenly on both sides while maintaining its shape.
- Drain on a piece of paper towel.

Potato Foam:
- Gently heat up the potato purée with the milk, cream and butter. Season to taste.
- When the potato has the consistency of whipping cream, place in a cream whipper charged with the gas and whip until creamy.

To Serve:

- Season and sear the loins in a hot pan and roast for approximately 7 minutes in a pre-heated 375° F oven, turning halfway through the cooking. Remove from the oven and allow to rest.
- In a hot pan, add the bacon and chopped onion and cook until the onions are soft. Add the shredded cabbage and cook for another 2 minutes.
- Place the potato ring onto the plate and half fill with the shepherd's pie. (Ramekins can be used if the potato rings are not made.)
- Arrange the cabbage in front of the shepherd's pie and place 4 slices of lamb on top. Finally, place the potato foam on top of the shepherd's pie.
- Add the chopped rosemary to the sauce and spoon a little of the jus around the lamb.

TUSCANY

Philipsburg, Montana | Ranch at Rock Creek
Granite Lodge
Executive Chef Josh Drage

Upon arrival at the Ranch at Rock Creek, you will be 30 to 50 miles from civilization, the lone exception being nearby Philipsburg, population 930. Surrounded by pristine mountains and meadows, clear lakes and streams, life revolves around activities in the unspoiled Montana big sky country while enjoying the finest luxury accommodations in Granite Lodge, individual cabins and the ultimate unforgettable 'glamping' (luxurious camping) experience in canvas cabins.

The ranch is designed to offer something for everybody. There's horseback riding, mountain biking, hiking, fly fishing, archery, stagecoach rides, viewing wildlife, clay pigeon shooting, and when you're ready to relax, the spa, pool and Jacuzzi await.

Indoor activities center in The Silver Dollar Saloon adjacent to the Granite Lodge and Spa. In this authentically western environment, you'll find a truly western bar with saddles for seating and a wealth of entertainment options including a four-lane bowling alley, billiard tables, a 14-foot HD video screen and viewing area with karaoke, shuffleboard, board games, cards and game tables, darts and more.

If you go in winter, you'll find a wonderland unlike anything you've ever experienced. There's cross country and downhill skiing, snowmobiling, ice skating, sleigh rides, snowshoeing and a host of winter fun in the lodge. The only thing you cannot do is "glamp" in the luxury tents as the cold weather is not conducive.

www.theranchatrockcreek.com | Tel: 1 877 377 8056

Braised Leg of Lamb
with Taggiasca Olives, Spelt Grain and Sauce Soubise

Preparation: 60 minutes | Cooking Time: 3-5 hours | Serves: 4-6

Ingredients:

Braised Lamb:
1 5-lb bone-in leg of lamb
1 btl red wine
1 pint veal stock
1 onion
3 carrots
3 Roma tomatoes
3-5 fresh thyme bundles
7 peppercorns
5 cloves
5 allspice (whole)
1 head of garlic (broken into cloves and peeled)
3 bay leaves

Soubise Sauce:
1-1/2 cups béchamel sauce
1/2 cup grated gruyère cheese
1/4 cup grated parmesan cheese
1 cup cooked puréed onion

Brussel Sprouts:
24 brussel sprouts
3 tbsp canola oil
1 tbsp liquid aminos*
1 tbsp water
1 tbsp butter

Spelt Grain:
2 cups spelt
6 cups water
1 onion
3 sprigs celery
braising liquid (reserved from braising the lamb)
pinch salt
ground pepper
3 tbsp olive oil

Method:

Braised Leg of Lamb:
- Peel carrots and cut into large pieces. Peel onion and quarter. Peel garlic and quarter Roma tomatoes.
- Add all ingredients to a Dutch oven except the veal stock.
- Add enough veal stock to come 3/4 of the way up the side of the leg. Cover and cook in the oven for three hours at 250° F.
- Uncover and continue to cook allowing the leg to brown nicely on the top. After it does, put the meat back into the liquid and allow the top to brown again. Keep repeating the process, developing flavor of the broth, until the meat falls off the bone when pulled.
- Remove the leg from the liquid, let cool. Strain the liquid, remove the fat, and reduce by half. Pick the meat from the bone and remove any unwanted parts. At this stage, the meat should be in nice 3 to 4 oz pieces. Let cool completely in the reduced braising liquid.

continued...

Braised Leg of Lamb
with Taggiasca Olives, Spelt Grain and Sauce Soubise

Soubise Sauce:
- To béchamel sauce add gruyère cheese, parmesan cheese, and onion. Add salt and pepper to taste.
- Heat until flavors are thoroughly blended and the sauce is smooth.

Brussel Spouts:
- Trim off the cut end of the sprouts, removing any loose leaves. Halve each sprout and set aside.
- In a large sauté skillet, heat the oil on medium-high heat. Add each sprout, cut side down, and let brown.
- Give them a couple flips and add the liquid aminos, water, and butter. Turn heat to low and continue to cook reducing liquid and glazing at the same time.

Spelt:
- Add the dry spelt and water to a sauce pot, cover, turn on low heat and cook for about 20 minutes until grain is nice and tender. Set aside to cool.
- Finely brunoise** the onion and celery and set aside

Accompaniments:
- Trim around the pit of the olive making nice petals.
- Fry a small handful of sage leaves in a canola/olive oil blend at 300° F until the leaves just begin to turn to a dark wet green. Remove from oil with a mesh, lay on a paper towel, sprinkle with salt and let dry.

To Serve:

- Cook the spelt ahead of time and let cool.
- Prepare the soubise sauce and keep warm.
- Ready all of the accompaniments.
- Cook the brussel sprouts.
- Reheat the servings of meat in a sauté pan with enough liquid to come up a third of the way around the meat.
- Heat and reduce the liquid to glaze the meat. Add an ounce of butter and toss in the sauté glazing nicely.
- In a separate pan, sauté the onion and celery until soft and add the spelt grain with a two ounce ladle of the braising liquid from the lamb. Add an ounce of butter and reduce the liquid by half, warming and glazing the spelt.
- Serve the lamb on top of the spelt and the soubise sauce on the side. It will not turn out well to place the sauce on the meat. Dress the sauce and plate with the accompaniments.

* Liquid Aminos is a certified non-GMO liquid protein concentrate, derived from soybeans. It is considered a healthy alternative to Soy and Tamari sauce.

** Brunoise is a culinary knife cut in which the food item is first julienned and then turned a quarter turn and diced again, producing cubes of about 1/8-inch or less. Technically, it is simply a very small dice.

POULTRY

Oracabessa Bay, Jamaica | GoldenEye

Fleming Villa
Chef Talcie Neil

As mentioned earlier, GoldenEye, originally home to Ian Fleming, is today a luxury retreat on the north shore of Jamaica just 20 minutes from Ocho Rios. Its numerous accolades from leading travel publications such as *Travel + Leisure, Condé Nast Traveler, Wall Street Journal, NY Times, Robb Report, Departures* and many others testify to the resort's idyllic setting, superb accommodations, fine service, and tasty cuisine.

Originally, GoldenEye was Fleming's paradise, his escape from worldly distractions where he could dream and create his classic James Bond series. Today, Chris Blackwell, decidedly creative in his own right having founded highly successful Island Records and other business ventures, now owns the resort and has developed it into one of the finest of its kind worldwide.

The Fleming Villa is all about privacy. Set aside from the main resort, it offers the ultimate in seclusion with its own pool, pool house, gardens, private beach, staff and menus prepared by the villa chef. While removed from it all, you are within easy walking distance of the spa, Bizot Bar, restaurants, water sports and other activities. It is a world unto itself filled with every pleasure.

This Jerk Chicken recipe is a favorite served at GoldenEye's two dining spots—Bizot Bar and The Gazebo—as well as in the privacy of the Fleming Villa's private dining room.

To read more about GoldenEye, see the Index by Hotel & Resort at the back of the book.

www.goldeneye.com | Tel: 1 800 OUTPOST

Jerk Chicken

Preparation Time: 1 hour | Cooking Time: 15-20 minutes | Serves: 2

Ingredients:

1 chicken
2 scotch bonnets or
   hot chili peppers
1 large onion
4 spring onions
10 whole allspice seeds
1 sprig of thyme
1 tsp brown sugar
salt to taste
2 tbsp oil
2 tbsp soya sauce

Honey Mustard Dip:
1 tsp mustard
2 tbsp honey

Method:

For the Chicken:
- In a food processor, combine all ingredients (except chicken) until they make a paste.
- Cut chicken in quarters.
- Wash and season chicken.
- Let marinate in the paste for about an hour.
- Grill and serve.

For Dip:
- Combine mustard and honey.
- Whisk together and serve with chicken.

Dorset, England | Summer Lodge Country House

The Restaurant
Executive Chef Steve Titman

Built in 1798 by the 2nd Earl of Ilchester, the house was enlarged in 1893 by the 6th Earl who commissioned his friend and author, Thomas Hardy—an architect by profession—to draft the plans. It was again updated in 1932 by the last Earl to live in Dorset when he brought his bride home to live at Summer Lodge. Margaret and Nigel Corbett then purchased the property in 1979, becoming only the second owners in nearly two centuries. In 1988, the stables and coach house were converted into bedrooms and an all-weather tennis court and heated pool were added. A few years later, the dining room was enlarged and remodeled to compliment the Thomas Hardy-designed drawing room.

In 2003, the hotel became part of the Red Carnation Hotel Collection, and a complete refurbishment followed. Today, this charming Relais & Châteaux member and winner of dozens of top awards from *Condé Nast, Trip Advisor, Wine Spectator* and others, receives guests from the world over.

Executive Chef Steven Titman, formerly at the White Barn Inn in Kennebunkport, Maine—one of the U.S.A.'s top 10 hotel restaurants—blends his creativity with a talented staff in keeping with the influences Beatrice Tollman, President and Founder of the Red Carnation Hotel Collection, who entrusts him with her famous signature dishes.

Summer Lodge can also provide maps of the best walking and jogging routes, arrange for picnics, complimentary paints, brushes and easels and a wide array of activities such as cycling, horseback riding, country walks, fishing, while for those interested in arts and crafts, needlecraft and antiques can explore the abundance of local specialty shops.

www.summerlodgehotel.co.uk | Tel: +44 (0) 1935 482000

Duck Cottage Pie

Preparation Time: 2 hours | Cooking Time: 40 minutes | Serves: 4-6

Ingredients:

2-1/4 lbs coarsely ground duck breast
3-1/2 tbsp clarified butter
1 tbsp tomato purée
1/2 tsp rubbed thyme
1 bay leaf, crumbled
1 tsp chopped sage leaves
2 stalks celery, finely chopped
1-1/2 Spanish onions, chopped
6 medium carrots, chopped
1 tsp parsley, chopped
1/2 tsp chervil, chopped
2 cups chicken stock
2-1/4 lbs cooked potatoes, flavored with cream and butter, salt and freshly-ground pepper

Method:

- Sauté onions in butter until translucent.
- Add duck meat and sauté until brown, stirring continuously.
- Add carrots, celery, tomato purée, parsley, chervil, thyme, crumbled bay leaf and sage leaves.
- Add chicken stock and season to taste with salt and pepper.
- Put meat mixture into a well-buttered deep, oval dish. Mash the cooked potatoes and add clarified butter, salt and pepper to taste.
- Pile the potato mixture on top of the meat, covering completely, and brown in oven at 355° F for about 10 minutes or until potatoes are golden brown and crispy.

KwaZulu-Natal, South Africa | The Oyster Box

The Grill Room
Executive Chef Kevin Joseph

Majestically situated on the eastern seaboard of KwaZulu-Natal with sweeping views of the Indian Ocean and direct beach access, The Oyster Box is one of South Africa's most popular and distinguished hotels. This award-winning five-star property features 86 individually-decorated rooms, suites and villas that are stylish, comfortable, and equipped with the latest high tech amenities.

There is easy access to the cosmopolitan center of Durban with its enticing shops, shopping centers, and the verdant Midlands framed by the striking Drakensberg Mountains.

Also nearby are game parks, lodges and the historical battlefields of the Zulu Wars, Shaka, Dundee, Churchill, and the Boers where you can see and hear more about the amazing events marking South Africa's recent past.

The hotel's Grill Room, Ocean Terrace, Palm Court Restaurant, Chukka Bar, Lighthouse Bar, Oyster Bar and Wine Cellar—under the creative direction of Executive Chef Kevin Joseph—boast a variety of dining and social offerings to suit a range of moods and tastes from casual cocktails to gourmet dining. Using only the freshest seasonal ingredients sourced from local vendors, the cuisine at The Oyster Box gives you the most delectable sampling of local flavors while being environmentally sustainable and supportive of the local community.

One of South Africa's greatest architectural treasures, the resort is set in lush indigenous gardens and includes a luxury spa with an extensive range of treatments and exquisite spa dining, well-equipped private fitness club, two swimming pools, and gorgeous terraces and gardens.

www.oysterboxhotel.com | Tel: +27 (0) 31 514 5000

Arthur's Chicken Curry

Preparation Time: 30 minutes | Cooking Time: 3 hours | Serves: 4-6

Ingredients:

2 organic chickens totalling 3-1/2 lbs, each cut into 5-6 pieces
1 cup vegetable oil
1 medium onion, sliced
5 tbsp medium-strength marsala curry powder*
1 clove garlic
1 larger ginger root
2 green chili peppers
2 tsp dried turmeric powder
1 tsp salt
handful of curry leaves (fresh or dried)
1 bunch fresh coriander
2-3 cinnamon sticks
3 cardamom seeds, slightly crushed
1 cup water or chicken stock
4 large potatoes, quartered
2 tomatoes, sliced
1/2 tbsp garam marsala**

Method:

- In a blender, combine the garlic, ginger, green chilis and blend into a paste.
- Heat the oil in a large thick casserole. Slice the onion and sauté until golden brown.
- Add 4 tbsp of the Marsala and the turmeric to the spice paste. Then add chicken pieces and mix well, adding the salt and braising until browned.
- Spread another 2 tbsp of spice paste on top of the chicken in the pot. Add most of the curry leaves and coriander, then the cinnamon sticks and cardamom seeds.
- Continue braising for another 30 minutes, then add another tbsp of the spice mix, and a little more liquid, if needed.
- After 1-1/2 hours, add the potatoes, and when slightly soft, add the tomatoes. Turn heat down to medium-low.
- When the potatoes are tender, add a little more fresh coriander and curry leaves. When both the chicken and potatoes are tender, stir in the Garam Marsala.
- Serve hot.

Can substitute regular curry powder.
**If you do not have garam marsala, mix well together 1/2 tsp cinnamon; 1/2 tbsp cumin; 3/4 tsp each ground coriander, cardamom, and black pepper; 1/4 tsp each of ground cloves and nutmeg.

WESTERN CAPE, SOUTH AFRICA | BUSHMANS KLOOF

THE HOMESTEAD
Executive Chef Floris Smith

Voted the No. 1 Resort and Safari Camp in Africa in *Condé Nast Traveler* USA's 2013 Readers Choice Awards, Bushmans Kloof Wilderness Reserve & Wellness Retreat is a splendid five-star ecological oasis located near Cape Town. Majestic views, open plains, invigorating outdoor activities, luxurious accommodations and award-winning Cape cuisine combine to create an unforgettable luxury wilderness adventure.

This five-star Relais & Châteaux lodge is renowned for its service and warm hospitality. It also offers a host of enriching, energizing and relaxing experiences such as evening nature drives, guided rock art walks, mountain biking, canoeing, fishing, archery, and four swimming pools. You can dine under the African stars in a range of breathtaking locations, savouring delicious organic cuisine created from local recipes using the freshest seasonal ingredients. Bushmans Kloof is well-known for its superb contemporary Cape cuisine and world-class facilities set in one of South Africa's finest natural heritage sites.

A predator- and malaria-free reserve, it is a sanctuary to many endangered species of fauna and flora and renowned as the "world's largest open air art gallery" with over 130 ancient Bushman rock art sites.

The riverside spa gazebo, inspired by unique holistic healing qualities special to the area, features ancient treatments complemented by indigenous rooibos (an African evergreen bush with leaves that are often used to make tea), flowers and plants. Koro Lodge, a fully-catered villa five minutes from the main lodge, offers the ideal private wilderness experience for groups of friends and families with children of all ages.

www.bushmanskloof.co.za | Tel: +27 (0)21 481 1860

Sesame Fried Chicken

Preparation Time: 20 minutes | Cooking Time: 20 minutes | Serves: 4-6

Ingredients:

1 whole chicken, about 3-1/2 lbs, cut in 8 portions
7 oz evaporated milk
8-1/2 oz butter
3 cups oil
1 egg

For the Sesame Coating:
10 tbsp toasted sesame seeds
1 cup flour
1 tsp poultry seasoning
2 tsp garlic powder
1 tsp ground ginger
4 tsp paprika
2 tsp salt
freshly ground pepper

Method:

- Combine the coating ingredients into a fine mixture.
- Whisk the egg together with the milk, and dip chicken pieces into the mixture. Shake off excess liquid and roll in sesame coating mix.
- Heat oil and butter together in a deep frying pan over a medium-high heat, making sure the oil is deep enough to cover the chicken pieces half way up.
- Start with the drumsticks and thighs as they take longer to cook.
- Fry for about 25-30 minutes or until golden brown on both sides. Try to turn just once as the coating is very delicate.

St Barth, Caribbean | Hôtel Le Toiny
Le Gaïac
Chef de Cuisine Sylvain Révélant

It's a colonial paradise high on a hill overlooking the sparkling azue-blue Caribbean. Named the top hotel in St Barth on *Condé Nast Traveler's* Gold List 2013, Hôtel Le Toiny's 15 recently-updated, pastel-hued Villa Suites reflect the island's famed French Colonial style. These residences are self-contained cottages that include 13 one-bedroom Villa Suites, one Junior Suite, and La Villa—a 1-3 bedroom Master House that includes two bungalows. Each offers ocean views, luxurious textiles, a kitchenette, large terrace and private heated swimming pool.

Private and discreet, this spectacular boutique retreat is set on 38-acres on the Island's southeastern side. Its exquisite Restaurant Le Gaïac, considered the best dining venue in St Barth, features innovative French cuisine with local flavors. Other amenities include the ocean view fitness center, Serenity Spa Cottage and a beach access path.

There is no shortage of things to do on St Barth. You can rent a car and circle the island in less than two hours. There are day trips to St. Maarten, St. Martin and Anguilla; catamaran excursions, sunset cruises, horseback riding and spending time shopping in the classy port town of Gustavia. If you are into water sports, the hotel can also arrange everything from scuba diving, surfing and beach picnics to deep-sea fishing.

www.hotelletoiny.com | Tel: +590 (0)590 27 88 88 | 1 800 680 0832 (from North America only)

Duckling Filet
with Caramelized Chicory Radish and Foie Gras Jus

Preparation Time: 1-1/2 hours | Cooking Time: 1 hour | Serves: 2

Ingredients:

1 duck, approx. 3 lbs
1 tsp olive oil
2 oz butter
1-1/4 cup chicory
3-1/2 oz red chicory
2 tsp radish
2 tsp black radish
3-1/2 oz orange juice
3-1/2 oz lemon juice
3 tbsp sugar
1 tsp olive oil
salt and pepper to taste

For the Jus:
2 cups bones
3 tbsp onions
1 tsp garlic
3 tbsp shallots
6 oz red wine
dash black pepper
1 bay leaf
1/2 tsp thyme
peanut oil
2 tbsp foie gras

Method:

Duck:
- Remove the legs, saving for another use.
- Remove the bones from remaining part of the duck and save for the jus.
- Combine the chicory, lemon and orange juice, salt and pepper in vacuum bag and cook sous vide* in water at 195°F for 30 minutes.
- Thinly slice the radishes and put in ice water. Clean leaves of red chicory.
- Make the duck jus. Wait to add the foie gras at the end when ready to serve.
- Brown the breast on the skin side, and finish the cooking in a 375°F oven for 8 minutes. Let meat rest for another 8 minutes.

Duck Jus:
- In a pan, lightly brown the bones in peanut oil and butter.
- Add onions, garlic, shallots, thyme, and bay leaf.
- Deglaze pan with red wine two times, continue to cook until wine has reduced.
- Cover bones with 3 quarts water and reduce to half a quart. Strain and discard solids.
- Add foie gras just before serving.

* Sous vide is a long-established cooking method that uses immersion of an air-tight plastic bag in hot water and cooking over a very low heat for a long period, resulting in some of the most tender, flavorful meat you've ever tasted. An easy technique, the air is sucked out of heat-safe plastic bags, i.e. those produced by FoodSaver.

County Laois, Ireland | Ballyfin
State Dining Room
Chef Ryan Murphy

Rich in history, gallantry and romance, Ballyfin dates back to ancient times, serving as the ancestral home of the O'Mores, Crosbys, Poles and Wellesley-Poles–family of the Duke of Wellington. The current manor, built in the 1820s by Sir Charles Coote, still displays his coat of arms above the entrance.

Nestled in 600 acres of spectacular gardens, grottoes, forests and natural lake, this palatial country house has long been deemed the most lavish Regency mansion in Ireland, and over the past decade, has been meticulously restored. Today, it showcases some of Ireland's finest architecture, furnishings, art and antique collections. Just 80 minutes from Dublin airport, Ballyfin embodies the gracious traditions of noble Irish hospitality.

Each of the 15 bedrooms is individually decorated with magnificent furnishings (as well as flat screen TVs, wireless Internet and other modern perks) while the public rooms display exquisite collections of 18th–20th century Irish art and antiques from the world over. An enormous saloon, eighty-foot library, elegant drawing room and sun-filled conservatory offer various settings for enjoyment and relaxation.

Indoor activities include a spa, gym, and indoor pool while an endless array of outdoor pursuits includes boating and fishing on the lake, clay pigeon shooting, falconry, tennis, archery, golf, and pony-drawn carriage rides.

Dining venues range from the grandeur of the State Dining Room or intimacy of the Van Der Hagen Dining Room to more casual locales such as the Library, Bar or Conservatory and private dining in the Porcelain Room lined with 'Flora Danica' china, or the dramatic Wine Cellar.

Chef Ryan Murphy, raised in New York City, arrived at Ballyfin from the Lowry Hotel in Manchester, England where he was Executive Head Chef, having previously been Chef de Cuisine at The Savoy's River Restaurant. Already one of Andrew Harper's 2013 Grand Award Winners as Hotel Restaurant of the Year and Best in Style 2011 from *Food & Wine*, Ballyfin is said to be well on its way to one or more Michelin Stars.

www.ballyfin.com | Tel: +353 (0) 5787 55866

Organic Chicken
With Pearl Barley

Preparation Time: 1 hour | Cooking Time: 1-1/2 hours | Serves: 4

Ingredients:

For the Chicken:
1 whole medium size chicken
1 tsp four spice*
1 oz chicken stock
2-1/2 oz crème fraîche
sea salt
fresh ground white pepper
scant 1/2 cup Brunoise - finely chopped celery, carrot, shallot, leek
1/2 tsp chives chopped
1/2 tsp parsley flax, chopped
2 qts white wine chardonnay
smoked paprika
olive oil
clarified butter

Chicken Sauce:
4 cups water
3 cups chicken stock
1-1/2 lbs chicken and tail bones
1/2 cup white onion, chopped
3-1/2 oz leeks, sliced
scant 1/2 cup carrots, chopped
1/3 cup tomatoes, chopped
2 cups veal stock
1 cup sherry vinegar
1 bay leaf
3 tbsp olive oil

Pearl Barley:
2-1/4 lbs of pearl barley
1 onion
1/2 clove of garlic
14 oz white wine
1 bay leaf
1 qt chicken stock (heated)
olive oil
salt and pepper to taste
2/3 cup shredded cabbage

Method:

For Chicken:
- Detach thigh and drumstick from body in one piece. Keep as much skin as possible.
- Expose the bone of the thigh and cut around under the bone to remove the bone and tendons from the meat. Repeat this procedure for the other thigh and leg.

To make the Mousse:
- Remove breasts from bone. Remove the inner fillet, tenders and loins.
- Use the tenders and loins to make the mousse. You will need 5 oz of meat.
- Be sure meat is cold before putting it in the food processor; otherwise place it in the fridge for 1 hour.
- In the food processor, add meat, four spice, salt, and mince the mixture to a thick paste.
- With food processor running, add chicken stock slowly, and then the crème fraîche. The mousse should be dense. Pass it through a drum sieve.
- Sweat up the brunoise until al dente and deglaze with white wine. Reduce, until wine color turns amber and most liquid has evaporated. Let it cool, add white pepper and add to mousse.

continued...

Organic Chicken
With Pearl Barley

- Place legs between sheets of baking paper and pound until thin.
- Spread mousse on one of the leg and thigh pieces skin side down. Repeat for the second leg and thigh piece and sandwich both pieces together. Wrap in cling film and refrigerate until required.

For the Chicken Breast:
- Remove the skin, season it with salt and pepper, then place on a baking tray, stretching with non-stick paper, bottom side up. Place another tray on top to keep flat.
- Cook in a pre-heated 320° F oven for 20 to 25 minutes until golden brown
- Coat the breasts with smoked paprika and olive oil then roll (from thin end of fillet) in cling film to make a sausage. Refrigerate.

To Complete:
- Place leg and thigh and the breast in a sous vide** water bath at 145°F for 1 hour. Afterward, season with salt and pepper.
- Brown the skin in a pan with oil and clarified butter. When hot, add chicken and cook 2-3 minutes until golden brown. Turn over and repeat.

For the Sauce:
- Heat oil in pot and just before it starts to smoke, add chicken bones and brown them. Let brown for 10 minutes, trying not to stir.
- Once browned, add all the vegetables (except tomatoes) and brown. Deglaze with 2 cups water, scrape pot and reduce until pot is almost dry and it turns to a glaze. Then deglaze with half the chicken stock. Cook and reduce until a glaze forms in the pot. Then deglaze with sherry vinegar and cook till another glaze forms. Add tomatoes and cook for 5 to 7 minutes, then add remaining liquid.
- While cooking, skim fat off top. Reduce sauce until there is 1-1/4 cups left. Strain through a chamois and whisk in olive oil to emulsify.

For the Barley:
- Sweat onions and olive oil. Once the onion is semi-translucent, add the barley and coat with olive oil.
- Heat until the barley has a hard coating and season with salt and pepper. Add 6 oz of hot chicken stock and allow to reduce, stirring continuously. Repeat this process four times until all the stock has been used and the pearl barley has a creamy consistency.
- Prepare cabbage by cutting into ribbons and blanch to al dente.

To Assemble:
- Slice chicken breast into 4 pieces, and slice leg into 4 pieces.
- Place one tbsp of pearl barley on left hand side of plate, taking another tbsp and drag a line of pearl barley from this mound across the plate.
- Place a large tbsp of cabbage on the mound of pearl barley, and place one piece of chicken breast on the mound. Place one piece of chicken next to the line of barley. Place the leg of chicken and the chicken skin in the center of the plate and dress with sauce.
- Garnish with edible flowers such as marigold and tatsoi leaves or as desired.

See Recipe Basics
**Sous vide is the immersion of the ingredients in an airtight, heat-proof plastic bag in hot water, first removing the air from the bag, i.e. those made by FoodSaver

Fish

Maui, Hawai'i | Four Seasons Resort Maui at Wailea

Ferraro's, DUO, Spago Maui
Master Executive Chef Roger Stettler

Maui's first and only Forbes Five-Star resort is nestled on 15 acres of breathtaking Wailea Coast. The 380-room oceanfront property is world-renowned for its comfortable opulence, impeccable service, luxurious amenities, and for living in harmony with its environment and community. The resort is also home to one of the nation's top-rated spas committed to wellness.

Three of Hawaii's most acclaimed restaurants—Ferraro's Bar e Ristorante, Spago Maui, and DUO, a premium steak and seafood restaurant—balance the sumptuous culinary offerings.

The Four Seasons Resort Maui caters to the needs and interests of all generations with world-class activities and one-of-a-kind *Unforgettable Events*, sports and cultural events not experienced elsewhere. A museum quality Hawaiian-inspired art collection, three pools overlooking the azure-blue Pacific, including an adults-only Serenity Pool with exclusive Missoni-designed cabanas, are just the beginning.

In 2013, the resort introduced a "going green" arrival option, with guests reserving Motor Trend's 2013 Car of the Year, the all-electric Tesla S 85 luxury sedan, to travel from the Kahului Airport to the resort and return. "From the moment guests step off the plane, they can begin embracing Maui's lush tropical setting—bedecked with dazzling flowers and fauna—without leaving a carbon footprint," said Mark Simon, the resort's marketing director.

The Four Seasons Resort Maui consistently receives accolades from noted national and international magazines, their readers and editors, and prestigious websites. The Virtuoso award selected by the editorial staff of *Virtuoso Life* magazine, *Condé Nast's* Platinum List, and *Travel + Leisure Magazine* all award high marks.

www.fourseasons.com/maui | Tel: 1 808 874 8000

Poached Ahi with Apple Fennel Salad

Preparation Time: 1 hour | Cooking Time: 20 minutes | Serves: 1

Ingredients:

6 oz ahi
2 oz roasted fingerling potatoes
2 oz spinach
3-4 basil leaves

Spinach Cream:
4 oz spinach
1 tbsp garlic
1 tbsp shallots
1 oz extra virgin olive oil
1 oz butter
2 oz cream

Garnish:
1-1/2 tsp fennel pollen*

Apple Fennel Salad:
2 oz apple
1-1/2 tsp curry
1 oz butter
2 tbsp shaved fennel

Lemon Vinaigrette:
2 oz extra virgin olive oil
1 tbsp lemon juice

Method:

Ahi:
- Cryo-vac** ahi with basil leaves and extra virgin olive oil. For medium rare, cook in sous vide water at 280° F for 7 minutes.

Spinach Cream:
- Sauté spinach with garlic and shallots in oil and butter. Purée the spinach in blender with hot cream. Adjust seasoning with salt and pepper. Mix sautéed spinach just before plate up.

Apple Fennel Salad:
- Pan roast apples in butter with curry until tender, but still firm. Cool to room temperature and slice thin. Mix with sliced fennel and lemon vinaigrette. Assemble plate as shown above.

*Finely powdered fennel seed can be substituted.
**Place fish in a cooking bag and remove all air. FoodSaver and other vacuum sealers work best.

FIVE STAR RECIPES FROM WORLD FAMOUS HOTELS & RESORTS

Ubud, Bali | Viceroy Bali
CasCades Restaurant
Chef Nic Vanderbeeken

At the exquisite Viceroy Bali, you'll enjoy superb service and fine dining at the award-winning CasCades restaurant which is ranked as one of the finest restaurants in South East Asia. Its contemporary French menu is served in an exceptional South Seas setting overlooking the Petanu River gorge, creating a feast for palate, mind, and soul.

For guests in the 25 posh villas, there is a luxurious spa and beauty centre—both with breathtaking vistas, a valley-top infinity pool, gymnasium, library, and boutique.

Ubud, just minutes from the resort, is one of Southeast Asia's most charming villages. Here you'll experience a leisurely, laid-back pace and colourful ambience of artisans, shops, galleries, and cosy cafes. Bali also has one of the world's most diverse and innvoative performing arts cultures.

Performances are often Balinese interpretations of stories from Hindu epics such as the *Ramayana*. Famous Balinese dances include *pendet, legong, baris, topeng, barong, gong keybar,* and *kecak* (the monkey dance).

www.viceroybali.com | Tel: +62 361 971 777

Lobster Palm Heart and Papaya Coulis

Preparation Time: 45 Minutes | Cooking Time: 10 Minutes | Servings: 2

Ingredients:

For Lobster:
1 16-oz lobster
3-1/2 oz lemon juice
2 tbsp butter
1 tbsp chopped red chili

For Coulis:
1 tbsp butter
1 tbsp cognac
4 oz papaya
3 oz tomatoes, skin and seeds removed
2 tbsp cream
salt and white pepper
pinch of cumin

For the Base:
4 green asparagus, boiled until tender
7 oz palm heart, sliced and grilled on both sides

Method:

For Lobster:
- Break the head and the clips off lobster and sear them in hot butter until brown. Deglaze with 1 tbsp of cognac. Add water and cover. Cook at reduced heat for 25 minutes until a nice color.
- Strain the juice, getting rid of all the lobster pieces. Squeeze 3-1/2 oz of lemon juice into the lobster juice.
- The lobster body must be char grilled. Cut your lobster body in two parts, lengthwise. Roll up and attach with a skewer.
- Brush lobster with spice butter made of 2 tbsp butter and 1 tbsp chopped red chili.
- Char grill lobster for 4 minutes. Brush with spicy butter again and finish in a 320° F oven for 2 minutes.

For Coulis:
- Cut 4 oz papaya and 3-1/2 oz of the skinned and seeded tomatoes.
- Cook them in the lobster juice. Add 2 tbsp of cream and boil for 5-6 minutes.
- Use a blender to mix everything thoroughly. Add salt and pepper to taste. The coulis is done.
- Serve immediately, using a scoop to make coulis balls.

To Serve:

Place two halved asparagus on a slice of the grilled palm heart. Top with lobster and coulis formed into balls with a scoop as shown in the picture.

BERLIN, GERMANY | REGENT BERLIN

FISHERS FRITZ
Chef de Cuisine Christian Lohse

A haven of tranquil elegance in the vibrant city, the Regent Berlin is located on beautiful Gendarmenmarkt square in the historical center of the capital and offers remarkable views of two 18th-century cathedrals as well as the old concert hall. The most important museums, numerous luxurious boutiques, the famed Friedrichstrasse shopping mile, as well as several of the most significant sights – including the Brandenburg Gate, Reichstag, and Opera – are only a stroll away.

This exquisite 5-Star luxury hotel houses 156 beautifully-appointed guest rooms which are among the largest in Berlin, 39 suites, and a spectacular presidential suite on the top floor. Many of the rooms, which combine classic elegance with high technology, also have balconies. Considered by *Condè Nast Traveller* to be one of the 'best places to stay in the world' and named the "Best Hotel in Germany" in the January 2012 edition of *Condé Nast Traveler Magazine*, this exceptional property embodies the ultimate in service, ambience and amenities.

At the hotel's Michelin 2-starred gourmet restaurant, Fischers Fritz, chef de cuisine Christian Lohse offers high-class fish and seafood specialties served at the table with exceptional presentation. The critically-acclaimed chef was awarded a Michelin star just six months after opening and continues to delight discerning diners with his creations. In fall 2007, Lohse's dedication to his craft and relentless pursuit of perfection placed him firmly at the forefront of Berlin's culinary world when he became the first Berlin chef in 13 years to merit 2 Michelin Stars. He has maintained his crown as Berlin's 2 Michelin-starred chef for his classic French cuisine with a contemporary twist for the sixth year running.

www.regenthotels.com/berlin | Tel: 0049 (0)30 20 33 8

WILD SEA BASS
WITH GRILLED VEGETABLES & FOAMED LOBSTER SAUCE

Preparation Time: 1 hour, 20 minutes | Cooking Time: 40 minutes | Serves: 4

Ingredients:

Fish:
1 sea bass (approx. 2 lbs)
2 tbsp olive oil

Fish Dough:
2 lbs flour
2 lbs sea salt
4 qts water

Foamy Lobster Sauce:
7 oz lobster shell
6 oz Noilly Prat
12 oz liquid cream
7 oz roasted vegetables
Maldon sea salt*, black pepper, brown raw sugar
Tabasco
dash of lime juice
1 tbsp tomato paste
6 oz olive oil
3-1/2 oz butter

Roasted Seasonal Vegetables:
About 14 oz of carrots, onions, celery, fennel, garlic, squash, mushrooms, etc.

Method:

Fish:
- Gut sea bass, wash, drain, and then salt from inside. Mix flour, sea salt, and water and prepare dough.
- Roll out dough and wrap sea bass. Bake in a preheated 365°F oven for 15 minutes, then let it repose for another 20 minutes.

Vegetables:
- Roast a selection of seasonal vegetables slowly in olive oil.

Foamy Lobster Sauce:
- Heat the olive oil in a pot, add 7 oz of the roasted vegetables, and season with sea salt and raw sugar while stirring continually. Keep remaining vegetables warm for presentation.
- Add tomato paste and lobster shell and let the mixture simmer for a short time.
- Add the Noilly Prat and reduce to half. Add the cream, bring to a boil, then reduce and simmer for 15 minutes.
- Pass through a fine sieve and pour into a mixer and mix with butter and some olive oil. Season to taste with lime juice, Maldon sea salt*, and Tabasco.

To Serve:
Prepare dishes with vegetables. Fillet sea bass right at the table and put on prepared dishes. Serve with the foamy lobster sauce.

A course gourmet sea salt from England frequently used to finish dishes.

County Clare, Ireland | Dromoland Castle

The Earl of Thurmond
Executive Chef David McCann

The story of Dromoland is a fascinating journey into history which is reflected today throughout the famed baronial castle and its surroundings. One of the most famous in Ireland, it dates back to the 11th century and has endured battles and reversals of family fortunes to become a magnificent resort occupying some 1500 acres with views of the Shannon and Fergus rivers.

In 1921, the IRA marked Dromoland Castle for destruction. Fortunately, the orders were reversed at the last minute at request of local IRA leaders in County Clare who insisted that current owners, the Inchiquin Lords, had been fair and benevolent in dealing with their tenant farmers.

After the death of the 15th Baron of Inchiquin in 1929, Dromoland was supported mainly by the personal wealth of his widow, Lady Ethel Inchiquin, an heiress whose portrait, painted by Herbert Draper, still hangs near the staircase in the castle hall.

The quadrangle of 28 guest rooms, built in 1736, is almost a century older than the rest of the five-star hotels in Ireland. Luxurious accommodations reflect a décor based on 18th Century botanical drawings complemented by plush upholstery designed by the French Fabric House Pierre Frey. Modern amenities include Interactive TV with music and movies-on-demand, broadband internet access and socket converters.

Dining options range from the award-winning Earl of Thomond restaurant to casual fare in the Fig Tree and snacks at the country club. The cocktail bar, with spectacular views of the county's lakes, is also a popular gathering spot. Also available for your pleasure is a beautiful spa.

Activity options include horseback riding, fishing, archery, falconry, clay shooting, tennis, walking tours, and for golfers a championship course designed by Irish golfing legend J.B. Carr and noted golf course architect Ron Kirby.

www.dromoland.ie | Tel: +353 61 368144

Roast Monk Fish, Potatoes & Peas

Preparation Time: 50 minutes | Cooking Time: 1 hour | Serves: 4

Ingredients:

Fish:
4 7 oz monkfish tails, cleaned and skinned
4 white peppercorns
zest of 1/4 lemon
pinch of each:
    coriander seeds
    cumin seeds
    fennel seeds
    sea salt

Potatoes:
3 rooster potatoes*
4 scallions, washed and sliced
3-1/2 tbsp butter
2 oz olive oil

Peas Garnish:
1 cup chicken stock
1 small onion, peeled and diced
2/3 cup petit pois
1 clove garlic, crushed
3-1/2 tbsp butter
4-5 leaves of baby gem,** finely sliced
1 tsp chopped chervil

Method:

Fish:
- Put all the seasonings in a pestle and mortar and crush.
- Preheat oven to 355° F. Heat a non-stick frying pan, season the fish and brown on all sides. Place in the oven for approximately 8 minutes. Remove and rest.

Potatoes:
- Bake potatoes in the oven; then let rest for 10 minutes. Cut in half and scoop out all the pulp into a large bowl. Season with salt and pepper, butter, olive oil, scallions and mix well. Cover and keep warm.

Peas Garnish:
- Heat a heavy pot and add the onion, chicken stock, butter and garlic and saute until golden. Add the peas and bring to a boil to emulsify. Cover and keep warm.

To Serve:
- Place potatoes in the center of the plate. Slice one monk fish (or leave whole) and place on top of potatoes. Finish by spooning the pea garnish around the plate.

* Roosters are red skinned with yellow flesh. Can substitute red or white potatoes with creamy white flesh.
** Baby romaine or other crisp leaf lettuce.

FIVE STAR RECIPES FROM WORLD FAMOUS HOTELS & RESORTS

Guernsey, England | The Duke of Richmond

Leopard Restaurant
Head Chef Jack Darbyshire

Overlooking Cambridge Park and St. Peter Port harbor, The Duke of Richmond Hotel is perfectly located for the most enjoyable stay on the island of Guernsey. Extensively refurbished and reopened in May 2012 as part of The Red Carnation Hotel Collection, The Duke of Richmond offers 73 luxuriously appointed air-conditioned rooms and suites, many featuring panoramic sea views.

The delightful, peaceful location overlooks a quiet park and offers views of the sea and neighboring islands of Herm and Sark. The hotel is just up the hill from the bustling town center and an easy stroll to the harbor and thriving financial district.

The Residents' Lounge area boasts a strikingly contemporary black-and-white color scheme and is perfect for reading or just relaxing. Afternoon tea is also a highlight as is lingering over a couple of evening drinks.

Meals are served throughout the day in the South African-themed Leopard Bar and Restaurant. You can also enjoy the magnificent conservatory and outdoor terrace which offers superb views perfect for al fresco dining. Complimentary Wi-Fi is available throughout the hotel, and leisure facilities include a heated outdoor swimming pool and sun deck for tanning and relaxation.

www.dukeofrichmond.com | Tel: +44 (0) 1481 72622

Prawn Stroganoff

Preparation Time: 20 minutes | Cooking Time: 20 minutes | Serves: 4

Ingredients:

1-3/4 lbs shrimps, shelled and deveined
3-1/2 tbsp butter
1/4 cup minced onion
8 oz mushrooms, quartered
1 tbsp plain flour
1 tbsp brandy
1 tsp Worcestershire sauce
juice of 1 lemon
3/4 cup sour cream
3/4 cup double cream *

Method:

- Sauté the shrimp in a large skillet until lightly browned. Remove from skillet.
- In the same pan, sauté onion until soft, then add the mushrooms and cook until browned.
- Sprinkle the flour over the mushroom mixture and cook for 2 minutes.
- Reduce heat to medium-low and add the brandy, Worcestershire, and lemon juice.
- Add the shrimp, sour cream and double cream.
- Add salt and pepper to taste and stir mixture and cook about another 3 minutes or until the shrimp is cooked through. Be careful not to boil or overcook.
- Serve with rice.

Double cream has an approximate 48% fat content. You can substitute heavy cream or heavy whipping cream which are about 40% fat. The higher the fat count, the better.

Ravello, Amalfi Coast, Italy | Palazzo Avino

Ristorante Rossellinis
Executive Chef Michele Deleo

Set high on the Amalfi Coast with spectacular vistas of the glistening blue Mediterranean, Palazzo Avino offers a dreamy escape into a world of pure beauty and luxury. Below is the charming little town of Ravello built on the steep hillside, and completing this postcard setting are the pastel houses surrounded by landscapes of bright flowers.

Built in the 12th century as a villa for an important noble family, Palazzo Avino has been refurbished to the highest standards while retaining its impressive medieval and baroque features. There are 11 junior and deluxe Suites with sea views (some with terraces), 32 double rooms with sea and mountain views, each decorated in a different style with exquisite 19th century furnishings. The hotel's many International accolades include being named as one of the best hotels in the world by both *Travel + Leisure* and *Condé Nast Traveler* magazines.

Among several dining venues—all with spectacular Mediterranean views—is the Michelin 2-starred Rossellinis Ristorante featuring the finest Italian haute cuisine. A new addition to the Terrazza Belvedere, which serves a lighter fare, is the Lobster & Martini Bar where you can enjoy fresh local lobster paired with Champagne, Prosecco or your choice of 65 different martinis crafted by the palazzo's martini mixologists.

Additional amenities include a swimming pool, full service spa in a garden setting, gym, and a rooftop solarium with two whirlpool baths.

Palazzo Avino (formerly Palazzo Sasso) recently added a Clubhouse by the Sea just 15 minutes from the hotel. A complimentary private shuttle takes you to the seaside setting where you can enjoy a casual restaurant featuring the fresh catch of the day and pizza, plus a lounge, changing rooms and a small outdoor pool.

www.palazzoavino.com | Tel. +39 089 81 81 81

King Lobster
on Pizzaiola with Eggplant Caviar & Ricotta Ragu

Preparation Time: 2 hours | Cooking Time: 2 hours | Serves: 1

Ingredients:

King Lobster:
1 King Lobster, 21 oz

Bread "Pizzaiola" Style:
1/2 cup stale bread cut in small pieces
1/2 cup peeled plum tomatoes
2 tbsp fresh onions
1 tsp fresh garlic
2 tsp chives
1/2 rounded tsp dried oregano
1-1/2 tbsp fresh basil
2 tbsp extra virgin olive oil
salt and pepper to taste

Buffalo Ricotta Ragu:
3-1/2 oz ricotta cheese
2 tbsp cream
2 tsp milk

Eggplant Caviar:
5-1/2 oz violet eggplants
2 tsp garlic confit *
1 tsp fresh thyme
1 tsp marjoram
1 tsp ginger
scant 1/2 tsp lime zest
2 tsp brown sugar
scant 1-1/2 tbsp extra virgin olive oil
2 tsp soya sauce
salt and pepper to taste

Method:

Lobster:
- Cook in abundant salted water for about 5 minutes then cool in a water and ice bath.
- Remove the shell and save for plate decoration.

Bread "Pizzaiola" Style:
- In a large pan, fry oil, onions, and garlic, then add the tomatoes and all the aromatic ingredients. Cook for around 20 minutes.
- Add the stale bread in small pieces and stir all the ingredients. Then place in a preheated 355° F oven for around 5 minutes.

Eggplant Caviar:
- In a large pan, fry the eggplants whole. Then wash to remove excess oil and dress with the olive oil, thyme, marjoram, mashed confit, and cook in the oven for 30 minutes at 300° F.
- When done, scoop out the inside part of the eggplant and stir mix with the remaining ingredients. Divide in small pieces (like caviar).

Buffalo Ricotta Ragu:
- Stir all the ingredients and keep it cold in the fridge.

To Assemble:
- On the bottom of the plate, place Bread "Pizzaiola" Style.
- Then lean the King Lobster against part of the shell.
- Add the Eggplant Caviar, Buffalo Ricotta Ragu and an edible flower for decoration.

* Garlic Confit - see Recipe Basics

London England | The Chesterfield Mayfair

Butler's Restaurant
Executive Chef Ben Kelliher

The Chesterfield Mayfair is the original Red Carnation Hotel and a firm favorite with its regular guests. Standing graciously in the heart of Mayfair and Berkeley Square, the four-star luxury hotel epitomizes Mayfair chic and is cherished for its proud traditional British heritage.

The 94 deluxe guest rooms and 13 luxurious suites offer a range of styles to suit every taste from cosy comfort to extravagant elegance. Bedrooms are furnished with fabrics reminiscent of nearby Savile Row, the florals of an English cottage garden, or the vibrancy of the African savannah. All guest rooms, suites, and public areas have access to complimentary high-speed internet.

As for dining, the bright Conservatory provides an airy setting for cocktail parties and light lunches while Butler's Restaurant is renowned for serving "the best Dover Sole in London." For an early evening retreat, the Terrace Bar provides the perfect setting.

You can easily explore central London on foot. The glittering shops of Bond Street, Regent Street, and Piccadilly are just a few minutes away. To the south, the Royal Parks offer an inviting stroll towards Buckingham Palace for the Changing of the Guard. Nearby attractions include the Royal Academy of Arts, Burlington Arcade, and Fortnum & Mason—all situated on Piccadilly. A little further to the east are Soho and London's vibrant Theatreland, Big Ben, the Houses of Parliament, and the London Eye—a giant ferris wheel on the South Bank of the River Thames.

www.chesterfieldmayfair.com | Tel: +44 (0)20 7491 2622

Dover Sole

Preparation Time: 10 minutes | Cooking Time: 15 minutes | Serves: 1-2

Ingredients:

1 freshly-caught Dover sole
olive oil
salt and pepper
lemon garnish

Method:

- Clean and de-scale the sole.
- Lightly season the sole with salt and pepper then dust with flour.
- Brush each side with 1 tbsp olive oil.
- Place on a hot, char-grill or ridged grill pan for about 90 seconds.
- Carefully turn 90 degrees on the same side for another 90 seconds to form diamond markings.
- Turn over with a large metal spatula and repeat on the other side.
- Place sole in a baking dish and bake in a 350° F oven for 8-10 minutes. Fish is done when flesh moves easily away from the bone when separated by a fork.

PROVENCE, FRANCE | TERRE BLANCHE
FAVENTIA

Terre Blanche in eastern Provence is one of the most scenic and tranquil destinations in France. Here, at the gateway to the sunny French Riviera, is a family haven offering fabulous golf, fine dining, a myriad of activities and interests for all family members, and fabulous views of the perched villages of Pays de Fayence.

The 5-Star luxury resort offers 115 beautifully furnished independent suites and villas—all with the high-tech amenities and safes large enough to hold laptop computers. Spacious marble baths feature a tub, separate shower, double sink, marble mosaics and heated floors.

The four restaurants, offering different cuisines and atmospheres, include the poolside Tousco Grill, the jazzy Gaudina in the main building, and Les Caroubiers with its stunning views of the golf course. For a memorable gastronomic experience, Faventia is as must. All feature the freshest local produce and distinctive Provençal and Mediterranean flavours. Terre Blanche even has its own bakery which produces a delectable variety of home-made breads and pastries which are served in all the restaurants and suites. Also look for a mouth-watering selection of home-made jams, nougats, calissons, caramels and macaroons.

The two golf courses, designed by Dave Thomas, blend beautifully into the natural landscape of hills and valleys. Terre Blanche was chosen to host the Ladies European Tour Access Open Series and the only France-based event of the European Senior Tour. Golf instruction at the Académie David Leadbetter is open to all ages and skill levels.

Other activities include a spa, two tennis courts, a petanque court and swimming pool. The kiddies, ages 2-12, have their own wonderland of activities. Supervised by a qualified, friendly staff, children discover a world of water-based activities, two playrooms to challenge their imaginations, workshops, and exploring the outdoors. A video games room and a lounge with home cinema round off the offerings.

www.terre-blanche.com | Tel: +33(0)4 94 39 90 00

FIVE STAR RECIPES FROM WORLD FAMOUS HOTELS & RESORTS

Glazed Turbot with Glazed Peas 'André Moreau'
and Fresh Pea Falafel with Mint and Cilantro chutney

Preparation: 60 minutes | Cooking Time: 3-5 hours | Serves: 8

Ingredients:

Turbot:
9-11 lbs freshly caught turbot
2 tsp salt per pound of fish
1/2 tsp sugar per pound of fish

Fish Stock (glaze):
Head and bones from one turbot
1/2 cup shallots
2 cups white wine
3 qts water
3/4 cup butter
juice of 1/2 lemon

Moillee Sauce:
3/4 tsp mustard seeds
1/2 tsp dried green curry leaves
6 garlic cloves
3 tbsp fresh ginger root
1/2 small red chili
1/4 cup shallots
1/4 tsp turmeric powder
3 cups coconut milk
salt and pepper to taste
1 tbsp olive oil

Mint and Cilantro Chutney:
1/2 cup fresh coriander/cilantro
1-1/2 tbsp fresh mint
1 garlic clove
dried green chili to taste
1/4 cup yogurt
1/2 tsp lemon juice
4 cups water
1 tbsp salt
salt and pepper to taste

Fresh Pea Falafel Kromeskies (Croquettes):
(Serves 3)
3-1/3 cups fresh peas
2 tsp finely chopped garlic
1/4 cup white onions (finely chopped and sautéed)
2 tsp sesame seeds
1-1/2 tsp cumin powder
1/2 tsp baking powder
2 tsp minced parsley
2 tsp minced cilantro
1 egg
2/3 cup fine, dry black bread crumbs
salt and pepper to taste

Mousseline de Petits Pois (Lightly Whipped Fresh Pea Purée):
1 lb fresh peas
2/3 cup butter
salt to taste

Pea and Green Apple Salad:
3-1/4 cups cooked peas
1/4 cup diced red onion
1/2 cup pea shoots
1 granny smith apple (cut into julienne strips)
2 tsp fresh mint
2 tsp cilantro
1/4 cup white Chardonnay vinegar
1/4 cup olive oil
salt and pepper to taste

continued...

FIVE STAR RECIPES FROM WORLD FAMOUS HOTELS & RESORTS

Glazed Turbot with Glazed Peas 'André Moreau'
and Fresh Pea Falafel with Mint and Cilantro Chutney

Method:

Turbot:
- Clean and filet the turbot, then marinate for 14 minutes in 2 tsp of salt and 1/2 tsp of sugar for every pound of fish.
- Rinse and pat dry. Slice fish into steaks about 4 inches long weighing about 4 oz each.
- Wrap each steak in plastic wrap.
- Cook 'sous-vide' (inside an airtight plastic bag placed in simmering water) for 1 hour at about 100°F.
- Chill before removing turbot from bag.

Fish Stock (glaze):
- Combine bones, shallots, white wine and water. Simmer for 20 minutes, skimming regularly.
- Strain through a muslin cloth.
- Reduce to a glaze then beat in the butter.
- Add a few drops lemon juice.
- Beat to form an emulsion, then use as a glaze for the turbot steaks, spreading with a basting brush.

Moillee Sauce:
- Heat olive oil in a skillet. Add mustard seeds and roast until golden.
- Add curry leaves, garlic, ginger (finely chopped), chili and minced shallots. Simmer on low heat.
- Add turmeric, then coconut milk. Simmer for 20 minutes then strain through a fine sieve.
- Adjust seasoning and then work up to form an emulsion. Serve in a saucepot.

Mint & Cilantro Chutney:
- Bring water and salt to a boil, add cilantro leaves and cook until reduced to a pulp. Add the mint, cook for another five seconds, then remove from heat. Strain and chill.
- Add the remaining ingredients and combine in a food processor. Add salt and pepper if necessary.
- Set aside in an icing pipette.

Mousseline de Petits Pois (Lightly Whipped Fresh Pea Purée):
- Shell peas then flash-boil in salted water until tender. Strain, add to food processor, then pass through a sieve.
- Beat in the butter and adjust seasoning as necessary.

Fresh Pea Falafel Kromeskies (Croquettes):
- Shell peas then flash-boil in salted water until tender.
- Remove pea skins then mix a little more than 3/4 cup of the pulp with remaining ingredients.
- Mash with a fork, mold the falafel mixture into 1 inch balls and coat with the bread crumbs.
- Deep fry at 325°F.
- Serve one on the plate, two in a napkin.

Pea and Green Apple Salad:
- Remove skins from 1 cup of the cooked peas then mix pulp with the diced onion.
- Add the apple, followed by the pea shoots, mint, cilantro and oil. Adjust seasoning to taste.
- Serve in medium-size bowl.

To Serve:
- Plate as shown in photo.

PASTA

Ubud, Bali | Viceroy Bali
CasCades
Executive Chef Nic Vanderbeeken

The Viceroy Bali is an oasis for those seeking tranquility and serenity in the natural beauty of a mystic land. Set high on a mountain ridge overlooking the Petanu River and Valley of the Kings, total pampering is also part of the luxurious, authentic Balinese experience. There are just 25 villas in exquisite Balinese décor, each with its own private pool, splendid views and every amenity.

Activity options include the Lembah Spa and Beauty Centre which offer a full range of treatments that blend the best of Western wellness techniques with Balinese traditions handed down through the centuries. There's also a valley-top infinity pool, boutique, gym, Jacuzzi, cold pool and steam room.

Dining in the award-winning CasCades restaurant offers a refined French-inspired menu of the freshest ingredients with delicate influences of Japanese, Thai and Balinese flavors. The Viceroy Bar, with numerous awards of its own for its outstanding wine list and fully-stocked bar, is also completed by magnificent views.

Once a retreat for royals, the resort today offers the perfect setting for total privacy, relaxation and renewal as well as an excellent menu of activities, adventures and experiences of Indonesian art and culture in nearby Ubud. An eclectic town of 30,000 surrounded by forests and rivers, rice paddies and steep, narrow valleys, Ubud is one of Bali's most distinguished cultural centres. Its sophisticated art forms, including paintings, woodcarvings and handcrafted goods are complemented by its Balinese performing arts that often portray stories from Hindu epics. Among the most noted Balinese dances are *pendet, legong, baris, topeng, barong, gong keybar,* and *kecak* (the monkey dance).

One small point when you go. The Balinese eat with the right hand as the left is considered impure—a common belief throughout Indonesia. They will not offer or accept things with the left hand and would never use it to wave at anyone.

www.viceroybali.com | Tel: +62.361.971.777

Vegetarian Cannelloni
with Frisée Salad

Preparation Time: 1 hour | Cooking Time: 10 minutes | Serves: 1

Ingredients:

For Pasta Dough:
1 oz flour
1 egg
1-1/2 oz olive oil

Vegetables:
1 capsicum (red pepper)
1 zucchini
1 small eggplant
1 tsp ground cumin

Cannelloni:
2 oz ricotta cheese
1 rounded tbsp parmesan
5 oz olive oil
1/4 cup sundried tomato (preserved in oil)
1 tsp sugar

Frisée Salad:
2/3 cup frisée greens
juice of 1 lemon
1 tsp chopped rosemary

Method:

Vegetables:
- Blacken the capsicum on a grill, remove skin and seeds, and julienne together with the zucchini and eggplant.
- Sauté in very warm oil. Add salt, pepper and cumin.

Pasta Dough:
- Make a pasta dough by mixing flour, egg and olive oil.

Cannelloni:
- Roll pasta dough into thin layer and cut into four slices.
- Fill each with sautéed vegetables. Top each with the ricotta and parmesan and roll into four cannelloni. Cook in the oven at 350° F for 10 minutes.
- Blend the sundried tomato with the olive oil and sugar. Warm and spoon over cannelloni.

Salad:
- Prepare frisée salad and toss with lemon juice, salt, pepper and one spoon chopped rosemary.

FIVE STAR RECIPES FROM WORLD FAMOUS HOTELS & RESORTS

Guernsey, England | Old Government House Hotel / Spa

The Brasserie Restaurant
Executive Head Chef Stamatis Loumousiotis

In the heart of Guernsey's capital, The Old Government House is the most famous hotel in the Channel Islands—steeped in history and affectionately known as The OGH. The five-star property retains its original grandeur and provides gracious personal service to match.

Situated just up the hill from the main shopping street and barely a five-minute walk from the picturesque quayside, the ambiance is extremely peaceful and tranquil, despite its central location. On a quiet, charming street, the imposing Victorian façade overlooks a delightful little park. The property is arranged around a magnificent private garden, with manicured terraces and a heated swimming pool. Facing southeast, it is a perfect sun-trap that provides stunning panoramic views over the harbor, castle and sea. The islands of Herm and Sark are just a few miles offshore, and you can even view the faint outline of the French coast on a clear day. It is a truly idyllic spot for relaxing with a book, enjoying a cool drink, taking a dip and ordering a bite to eat.

The Brasserie provides an informal setting for breakfast, lunch and dinner. Daily specials feature the freshest local ingredients, delicious steaks and fresh Guernsey fish. The Curry Room offers authentic Indian cuisine in relaxed and convivial surroundings, or you can also dining al fresco in The Olive Grove on those warm, sunny days.

www.theoghhotel.com | Tel: +44 (0) 1481 724921

Pasta Primavera

Preparation Time: 1 hour | Cooking Time: 15-20 minutes | Serves: 2-3

Ingredients:

1 heaping cup broccoli florets
4 small asparagus spears
4 baby carrots cut in 1-inch pieces
1/2 cup frozen peas
8 baby onions
8 oz linguine
1 small zucchini, sliced thin
6 baby mushrooms, halved
3 minced garlic cloves (or to taste)
4 tbsp butter
1/4 cup chicken (or vegetable) stock
1/2 cup double cream
1/2 cup grated parmesan cheese
8 cherry tomatoes, halved
12 basil leaves, shredded

Tomato Sauce:
1 small onion, diced
1 clove garlic, minced
1 14-oz can chopped plum tomatoes
1 bay leaf
salt and pepper to taste

Method:

- Fill a large bowl with iced water.
- Boil the broccoli and asparagus for 1 minute, drain, and plunge into iced water. When cool, drain in a colander. Repeat process with carrots, peas and baby onions.
- Cook pasta until al dente.
- Heat the butter in a large sauté pan over a medium-high heat. When butter has melted, add the zucchini and mushrooms and sauté. Add the garlic and cook for another minute, stirring frequently. Pour in the stock then increase the heat, bringing to a boil.
- Add the cream and one half cup of tomato sauce, then the drained vegetables and linguine.
- Reduce heat until mixture is just simmering. Stir in the parmesan and combine to form a thick sauce. If sauce is too thick, add some stock or cream.
- To finish, add the cherry tomatoes and shredded basil. Stir in remaining tomato sauce and serve in a large pasta bowl, garnished with a sprig of basil.

For the Tomato Sauce:
- Brown onion and garlic in 2 tbsp olive oil. Add the tomatoes, season with salt and pepper, add a few peppercorns, and 1 bay leaf
- Cook over a medium-low heat until sauce has reduced to a think consistency.

LONDON, ENGLAND | THE MONTAGUE ON THE GARDENS

THE BLUE DOOR BISTRO
Executive Chef Martin Halls

Located next to the British Museum in Bloomsbury, The Montague is just a short walk from Covent Garden, Oxford Street and the Theatre District. This stylish, long-established Georgian townhouse which gives you the feeling of being in a charming country home, overlooks its own private garden in the heart of one of the most beautiful and fashionable areas of central London.

The hotel's 88 exquisitely appointed rooms and 11 suites offer an enchanting variety of different styles, each with independent air-conditioning, complimentary Wi-Fi and other amenities. Elegantly understated, the rooms are furnished with exquisite fabrics capturing the timeless elegance of Bloomsbury and its literary heritage.

Consistently voted one of London's top hotels by *TripAdvisor*, both the hotel and its Blue Door Bistro restaurant have earned numerous accolades.

Specializing in modern European cuisine created with the freshest of seasonal ingredients and herbs from the hotel's own herb garden, The Blue Door Bistro is one of the most popular dining spots for locals as well as visitors. Using classical techniques, the chef and his team prepare superb seasonal British menus. The dishes, such as the Tuna Spaghetti on the next page, also incorporate the creativity of Beatrice Tollman, President and Founder of the Red Carnation Hotel Collection who, herself, is an avid chef.

The dishes may also be enjoyed al fresco on the delightful terrace, while during the summer months the Montague Wood Deck is the setting for sizzling barbecues and spit roasts. And every December, the deck is transformed into The Montague Ski Lodge complete with caroling and falling snow. You can also enjoy the Montague's legendary afternoon tea in the Conservatory, enjoy a Cuban on the Cigar Terrace, or relax in the cosy Terrace Bar.

www.montaguehotel.com | Tel: +44 (0) 20 7637 1001

Tuna Spaghetti

Preparation Time: 1 hour | Cooking Time: 1 hour | Serves: 8

Ingredients:

1 14-oz can of plum tomatoes, chopped
16 oz canned tuna in oil
1 small onion, chopped
2 cloves garlic, chopped
1/4 cup Niçoise olives
8 oz spaghetti
olive oil
3-1/2 oz can anchovy fillets (optional)

Method:

- Sauté the onions and garlic over a medium heat until translucent.
- Add tomatoes, reduce heat and simmer for 30 minutes.
- Add tuna, olives and anchovy fillets. Season with salt and pepper to taste.
- Cook spaghetti until al dente. Drain well, then toss in a warm pan with a little olive oil.
- Pour in half the sauce and toss again.
- Put mixture into a large pasta bowl and top with remaining sauce.

Chef's Tip: This dish is good hot or cold.

Umbria

DESSERTS

County Mayo, Ireland | Ashford Castle
George V Restaurant
Chef Stefan Matz

Situated in a magnificent 350-acre estate on the picturesque shores of Lough Corrib, Ashford Castle is one of Ireland's most impressive award-winning five-star hotels. With a history stretching back almost 800 years and most recently home to the wealthy Guinness family, it provides lavish hospitality on an epic scale. Famous for its magnificent setting and attention to detail, Ashford Castle has become one of the most sought-after and romantic venues for fairytale weddings, supplying lasting memories for brides and grooms from around the world.

Each of the castle's 83 rooms and suites are individually designed. Many of the original features have been preserved, yet all are equipped with modern amenities including Wi-Fi and interactive TV.

Guests dine in the George V Restaurant, aptly named as it was built to host evening dinner parties for the former Prince of Wales. More informal dining is provided in the Cullen's Cottage Restaurant, while The Drawing Room serves light meals and snacks during the day and a magnificent traditional afternoon tea.

Activities include some of the best fishing in all of Ireland, as well as a splendidly-equipped falconry and equestrian center. Golfers can enjoy the estate's nine-hole, 2,996-yard par 35 parkland course. Being a very family-friendly property, Ashford Castle offers something for every age group including tennis, biking, clay pigeon shooting, archery, horseback riding, hawk walks, chess and backgammon, lake fishing, boat cruises and host of other water sports. You can also order luncheon picnic baskets to enjoy on the gorgeous estate. And, of course, the spa's health & beauty facilities offer total pampering.

For children and pre-teens, Ashford Castle also provides kids' bathrobes, slippers, a special children's menu and exceptional junior spa treatments.

www.ashford.ie | Tel: +353 94 9546003

Rice Pudding

Preparation time: 1 hour | Cooking time: 30 minutes | Serves: 4-6

Ingredients:

Pudding:
2-1/2 oz jasmine rice
1/2 cup sugar
1 vanilla pod
4 strips lemon peel
2 cups whole milk
1 cup double cream
2 cups double cream, whipped

Salty Caramel Sauce:
1-1/4 cup sugar
3-1/2 tbsp butter
1 cup double cream
1 tsp salt (or to taste)

Caramelized Nuts:
2 cups nuts including pecans, almonds, walnuts and pumpkin seeds
5 oz sugar

Method:

Pudding:
- Put all ingredients except the whipped cream in a saucepan. Cook over a moderate heat for about 30 minutes, stirring often to avoid burning, until rice is tender and all the water has been absorbed.
- Pour onto a flat dish and cover with cling film to prevent skin from forming and let cool.
- When completely cooled, fold in whipped cream.

Carmel Sauce:
- Put the sugar in a sauce pan and add enough water so it looks like wet sand, then boil until it reaches a caramel colour.
- Remove from heat, whisk in butter and cream. Return to the heat, bring to a boil and add salt.

Caramelized Nuts:
- Toast nuts in oven.
- In a wide pan or skillet, put the sugar and enough water so it looks like wet sand, and cook until mixture is on the verge of caramelizing.
- Turn off heat and add nuts, stirring vigorously. The nuts will crystallize, turning white as they become coated with sugar.
- Turn heat back on, stirring continuously to caramelize the individually crusted nuts.

To Serve:
Spoon pudding in small individual bowls and top with a small amount of warm caramel sauce.
Put remaining sauce in a small bowl and serve on the side with a bowl of the nuts.

Florence, Italy | Hotel Lungarno

Borgo San Jacopo
Chef Beatrice Segoni

With splendid views of Ponte Vecchio, the Arno River and the city's Renaissance architectural works, the luxurious five-star Hotel Lungarno immerses you in pure grandeur. Designed by Florentine architect Michele Bönan, there are 73 rooms and suites with every amenity. It also features the city's finest contemporary art collection with over 400 pieces including works by Cocteau and Picasso.

Here, you'll find fine Tuscan and Italian cuisines in its renowned gourmet restaurant, Borgo San Jacopo, where you look out onto a beautiful view of the Arno while chef Beatrice Segoni invites you to sample her delightful interpretations during lunch or dinner. Every menu is based on the purest of local ingredients including the finest Tuscan meats and cheeses, freshest fish and vegetables, as well as an extraordinary wine list consisting of over 500 prestigious labels.

The Picteau bar is the perfect place to enjoy coffee or a cocktail while surrounded by original art by Picasso and Cocteau. The terrace of La Terrazza lounge bar invites you for a drink on top of its medieval Consorti tower with views of the famous sights of Florence.

The White Iris Beauty Spa by Daniela Steiner offers a wide range of signature treatments inspired by the purity of nature and seductive simplicity of Florentine elegance. The "White Gold Treatments" are based on gold dust and pearls and are based on the most advanced scientific research.

www.lungarnocollection.com | Tel: +39 055 2726 4000

Parfait Vanilla Mousse with Canteloupe

Preparation Time: 2 hours | Cooking Time: 1 hour | Serves: 8

Ingredients:

18 oz milk
1 vanilla stick
6 egg yolks
1 cup sugar
1 tbsp powdered gelatin *
3 egg whites
3/5 cup of water
4 - 5 gelatin sheets *

Method:

Parfait of Vanilla Brûlée:
- In a bowl, mix the 6 egg yolks and sugar on low speed with an electric hand mixer or whisk until combined.
- Place the gelatin powder in a small bowl and stir in about 2 tbsp of water -- just enough to dissolve.
- Mix the milk and vanilla in a saucepan and heat until temperature reaches 175°F. Then add the softened gelatin.
- When the milk, vanilla and gelatin reach 175°F, return mixture to a bowl and place in the fridge to slightly cool. Once cooled, add the mixture of the egg yolks and sugar and return to fridge.
- When fully cooled, sprinkle sugar on top and burn slightly with a blowtorch.

Meringa Italiana:
- Combine 3/4 cup of sugar and 2 oz. of water in a small pan and bring to the boil, stirring continuously with a wooden spoon until the sugar dissolves to syrup consistency.
- Slowly whisk 3 egg whites with 1-1/2 tbsp of sugar until soft peaks form.
- Meanwhile, bring sugar syrup to 250°F until it reaches a hard ball stage. Beat on high with hand mixer or whisk and with the heat still on, gradually pour syrup into meringue. Beat at medium speed until cooled to room temperature. The consistency of the meringue should be thick and glossy.

Melon Gelatin:
- Peel cantaloupe. Dice enough to fill 1-1/2 cups and set aside. Chop and thoroughly blend the remainder in a blender.
- Pour the blended mixture into a saucepan and heat to 175°F-195°F. Then add 4 or 5 sheets of gelatin. Remove from heat when dissolved and place in the fridge until the mixture becomes a gelatin.

Presentation:
- Place the melon gelatin at the bottom of a round bowl. Then, add some of the diced melon on top. Add the Parfait of Vanilla Brûlée. Top with remaining melon gelatin shaped into a ball. Garnish the Meringa with some zucchini flowers on the side.

See Recipe Basics

County Clare, Ireland | Dromoland Castle

Earl of Thomond
Executive Chef David McCann

Dromoland Castle, one of the most famous baronial castles in Ireland, sits on 1,500 tranquil acres of lakes, ornamental grounds and woodlands with views of Shannon and Fergus from various locales. With numerous accolades including being named the No. 4 Resort in Europe in the 2013 *Condé Nast Traveler* Readers' Choice Awards, the staff spares nothing to provide you with every comfort.

The Staterooms and suites are unique in design and dimension, each with its own seating and dining area. The furniture throughout the castle complements specially commissioned design styles with fabrics by Colefax and Fowler and crystal and nickel lighting with wood bases harmonizing with the lines of the Louis XV furniture. Beautifully appointed bathrooms offer every luxury and feature marble and painted furniture. Amenities include interactive television with music and movies on demand, Internet access, and the castle's signature bathrobes and slippers. For the younger family members, the castle offers kids their own bathrobes, menus, children's TV and movies, and board games.

A wide selection of dining options include a la carte, gastronomic and daily table d'hôte menus. You can dine in luxury at the award-winning Earl of Thomond Restaurant in Clare or for a more informal setting, there's the Fig Tree restaurant. Afternoon tea is served in the drawing room and you can get a light snack at the Country Club. And for relaxation before dinner, unwind in the cocktail bar with its spectacular views of the lakes. You can also ask the chef to prepare special picnic baskets accompanied by a bottle of fine wine or chilled bottle of champagne.

Facilities include the pool, sauna, Jacuzzi, luxury health spa, and an 18-hole championship golf course. There's horseback riding, fishing, falconry, clay shooting, archery, tennis and more.

www.dromoland.ie | Tel: +353 61 368144

Crème Caramel with Mango

Preparation: 30 minutes | Cooking Time: 1 hour | Serves: 4

Ingredients:

Caramel:
1/2 cup caster sugar*
2-1/2 oz water
1 bay leaf
1 cinnamon stick

Custard:
2 cups milk
1 tsp vanilla extract
4 eggs
2 egg yolks
6 tbsp caster sugar

Mango:
1 mango, peeled and sliced
1 tbsp honey
1 tbsp water

Method:

Caramel:
- Place the sugar and 3-4 tbsp water in sauce pan with bay leaf, cinnamon and bring to a boil. Cook until syrup becomes golden brown.
- Remove from heat and whisk in remaining water. Remove the cinnamon and bay leaf and pour the caramel into the bases of four Dariole molds and set aside.

Custard:
- Preheat oven to 320°F.
- Warm milk and vanilla in sauce pan. Mix eggs, egg yolks and sugar together and whisk in warm milk.
- Pass mixture through a fine sieve, then pour egg custard into the molds and cover each with foil.
- Place the moulds in a deep tray pan and fill up half way with warm water. Place in the oven and cook gently until set -- approximately 40 minutes. Cool and chill.
- Loosen around the edges of the molds and release very carefully onto the serving dishes, allowing the liquid caramel flow around the base of each crème caramel.

Mango:
- Place ingredients in a sauce pan, bring to a boil, then reduce to a simmer until all the liquid has been reduced to a glaze. Cool and chill.
- To serve, spoon the mango around the base of each crème caramel.

Super fine sugar. See Recipe Basics.

London, England | The Chesterfield Mayfair

Butlers Restaurant
Chef Ben Kelliher

The Chesterfield Mayfair, the original Red Carnation Hotel Collection property, is in the heart of Mayfair and Berkeley Square within walking distance of Green Park, Piccadilly, Bond Street and Oxford Street. Also nearby are the designer shops on Savile Row, the West End theatre district, and the bars and restaurants of Soho and Mayfair.

Cherished for its proud, traditional British heritage, the hotel's 94 deluxe guest rooms and luxury suites offer a range of styles to suit every taste from cosy comfort to extravagantly elegant. Continually ranked high by *Condé Nast Traveler, Travel + Leisure, TripAdvisor* and others, the Chesterfield Mayfair is the epitome of British hospitality.

Butler's Restaurant, also known for "the best Dover Sole in London", offers elegant dining and excellent service, making it a popular favorite with local residents as well as hotel guests. Featuring fresh English cuisine with international influences, there are breakfast, lunch, dinner and a la carte menus plus a popular pre-theatre option. Creative vegetarian dishes are always a hit as are the scrumptious desserts that may include sticky toffee pudding with vanilla ice cream or Honeycomb Ice Cream featured on the next page.

The Conservatory provides a bright, airy setting for light meals and the hotel's award-winning afternoon tea. For pure relaxation after a day of shopping and sightseeing, you can relax in the intimate Terrace Bar.

The hotel also boasts an excellent wine cellar containing some of the world's great labels and vintages as well as an excellent offering of lesser known, but excellent wines. Also featured are distinguished wines from South Africa's celebrated Bouchard Finalyson winery.

www.chesterfieldmayfair.com | Tel: +44 (0)20 7491 2622

Honeycomb Ice Cream

Preparation: 1 hour | Serves: 8

Ingredients:

1 cup corn or glucose syrup
1 cup granulated sugar
1 tbsp white vinegar
1 tbsp baking soda, sieved
1 qt vanilla ice cream

Method:

- In a sauce pan, dissolve sugar, syrup and vinegar over a medium heat.
- Turn up heat and boil until syrup turns a light caramel colour.
- Remove pan from heat and quickly stir in baking soda.
- Pour mixture into a high-sided baking sheet lined with parchment paper and greased with butter.
- Set aside to cool and harden. Do not refrigerate.
- Once hardened, this brittle, crunchy slab becomes the honeycomb base.

To Assemble:

- Slightly soften the ice cream in a chilled ceramic bowl.
- Carefully break honeycomb slab into various sizes, no larger than 3/4 inch and quickly fold half of the pieces into the ice cream.
- Pour the ice cream into an ice cream mould or back into the original ice cream container and re-freeze.
- Keep the remaining honeycomb in an air tight container for topping when serving.

County Laois, Ireland | Ballyfin
State Dining Room
Chef Ryan Murphy

At the foot of the Slieve Bloom Mountains on 600 splendid estate acres is Ballyfin, acknowledged as the most lavish Regency mansion in Ireland. Rich in turbulent Irish history, the site dates back to ancient times before becoming the ancestral home of the O'Mores, Crosbys, Poles, Wellesley-Poles– family of the Duke of Wellington, and the Cootes.

The house, itself, designed by the renowned Irish architects Sir Richard and William Morrison, was built in the 1820s for Sir Charles Coote, whose family enjoyed the house for exactly one hundred years with a large team of servants to preserve the leisurely life of luxury portrayed in the Edwardian photographs capturing tea on the terrace and skating in the walled garden.

With the arrival of Irish Independence, the Coote family sold the estate to the Patrician Brothers who, for much of the 20th century, ran a school at Ballyfin. Afterwards, it fell into years of disrepair, the urgent need for attention becoming quite apparent with the collapse of the Gold Drawing Room ceiling, masonry falling off the façade and the Conservatory in a disastrous state, all of which inspired the Irish Georgian Society to organize a fund-raising campaign. Still the future of one of Ireland's finest houses was uncertain until Ballyfin was acquired by its current owners who began a complete restoration spanning nine years.

The 5-star luxury hotel reopened its doors in May 2011 and today showcases some of Ireland's finest architecture, furnishings, art and antique collections. Its 15 magnificent staterooms and suites are individually named and decorated with posh furnishings representing the best of Irish tradition. Indoor activities include a spa, gym, and indoor pool while an endless array of outdoor pursuits include boating and fishing on the lake, clay pigeon shooting, falconry, tennis, archery, golf, and pony-drawn carriage rides.

Dining venues range from the grandeur of the State Dining Room or intimacy of the Van Der Hagen Dining Room to more casual locales such as the Library, Bar or Conservatory and private dining in the Porcelain Room lined with 'Flora Danica' china, or the dramatic Wine Cellar.

www.ballyfin.com | Tel: +353 (0)5787 55866

Summer Strawberry Crumble

Preparation: 1 hour | Serves: 8

Ingredients:

For the Strawberry Mix:
1-3/4 lbs ripe strawberries
1/2 cup caster sugar*
4 tbsp strawberry water**
1-2/3 tbsp olive oil
4 tsp fresh lemon juice
pinch sea salt
1 tsp freshly-ground black pepper
2 sprigs fresh mint, cut into long thin strips
2 leaves fresh basil, cut into long thin strips

For the Crumble:
1-1/4 cup high gluten flour
1/2 cup caster sugar
3 tbsp brown sugar
3/1-2 oz unsalted butter, room temperature

Method:

- Slice the strawberries in half from top to bottom. Mix together all the other ingredients for the strawberry mix, then add the strawberries and let them marinate for eight to ten minutes.
- While the strawberries are marinating, mix all the ingredients for the crumble together in a food processor to form a dough. Place in the fridge until firm.
- Rub the cooled dough together with your hands until it flakes and crumbles start to form. If necessary put in a mixer to break it up. Once it has achieved crumble consistency, place it on a baking tray lined with silicone paper and bake in the oven at 375°F for eight to ten minutes until golden brown.
- While the crumble is still hot, cut out round sections of 3 inches in diameter with a cookie cutter. Let the discs cool before lifting.
- To assemble the dish, place the ring cutter on a plate. Place the marinated strawberries into the mould and gently lift the mould. Place the crumble disk on top.
- To finish, add a scoop of good quality vanilla ice cream or strawberry sorbet on top of the crumble before serving.

* Super fine sugar. See Recipe Basics.
** Made by mashing a large handful of strawberries and straining through a sieve.

Cape Town, South Africa | The Twelve Apostles Hotel & Spa

Azure Restaurant
Executive Head Chef Christo Pretorius

The award-winning Twelve Apostles Hotel and Spa is poised at the edge of the world. On one side, the majestic Twelve Apostles Mountains reach towards the heavens; on the other, the sun sets on breeching whales, playful dolphins, and crashing rollers of the Atlantic Ocean Marine Park. Here you can walk the wilderness trails of the Table Mountain National Park, part of the UNESCO World Heritage.

With 55 spacious, beautifully-appointed guest rooms, 15 luxurious suites and the breathtaking Presidential Suite, each individually-decorated guest room combines sophistication with simplicity, comfort and elegance. Wi-Fi is complimentary and you can utilize the business center or 16-seat cinema. The exquisite gardens and pool overlooking the sea offer pure relaxation and tranquillity. **You also enjoy daily complimentary access to the hydrotherapy pools, flotation tank and health bar at the spa as well as a daily complimentary shuttle to Camps Bay and the Victoria and Alfred Waterfront in Cape Town.**

The Twelve Apostles Hotel and Spa is repeatedly voted as one of Cape Town's best hotels and is a member of Leading Hotels of the World. The world-renowned Azure Restaurant serves inspired international cuisine featuring South African influences and only the finest local herbs, seafood and wines. The Leopard Room Bar and Lounge is an elegant and sophisticated cocktail bar with live music and breathtaking panoramic sunset views from the Terrace.

The newly-refurbished Spa at The Twelve Apostles has a sparkling white interior and is equipped with the finest innovations in spa luxury. Guests can enjoy a signature B|Africa treatment at the award-winning spa, relax in the manicure and pedicure salon, or explore the two outdoor mountain gazebos.

www.12apostleshotel.com | Tel: + 27 (0)21 437 900

BEA'S CHEESECAKE

Preparation: 45 minutes | Cooking Time: 2 hours | Serves: 12

Ingredients:

3 lbs Philadelphia cream cheese
6 eggs separated, room temperature
1-3/4 cups granulated sugar
1 vanilla bean, split and seeds removed
1 tbsp vanilla extract
16 oz sour cream
pinch kosher salt

Topping:
16 oz sour cream
1/4 cup sugar

Crust:
2-1/4 cups finely-ground digestive biscuit crumbs*
1/2 cup white sugar
3 oz butter, melted
1 tsp ground cinnamon (optional)

Equipment:
8-inch spring form pan or mould

Method:

Crust:
- Mix cracker crumbs, sugar, melted butter, and cinnamon until well blended.
- Press mixture into mould in a consistent, thin layer and bake at 375°F for 7 minutes. Cool, then chill for 1 hour.

Cake:
- Whip the cream cheese with half the sugar. Add egg yolks, vanilla seeds, vanilla extract, salt and sour cream and whip thoroughly, scraping the bowl frequently.
- Whip the egg whites with the rest of the sugar. Carefully fold the whites into the cheese mixture and gently pour into the graham cracker-lined pan.
- Wrap the bottom of the mould pan and place in a water bath. Bake in the oven at 375°F for one hour, then turn heat off and let sit in the oven for another hour.
- Remove, cool on a rack, then chill in the fridge for 12 hours.

Topping:
- Pre-heat the oven to 210°F. Mix the sour cream and sugar and top the chilled cheesecake. Bake for 20 minutes.
- Chill in fridge for 24 hours before serving.

*Substitutions: Graham Crackers, Breton Palets or Hobnobs.

Maui, Hawaii | Four Seasons Resort Maui at Wailea

Ferraro's, DUO, Spago Maui
Executive Pastry Chef Rhonda Ashton

Maui's first and only Forbes Five-Star resort is nestled on 15 acres of the breathtaking Wailea Coast. The 380-room oceanfront property is world-renowned for its comfortable opulence, impeccable service, luxurious amenities, and for living in harmony with its environment and community.

The resort is home to one of the nation's top-rated spas committed to wellness. Three of the island's most acclaimed restaurants—Ferraro's Bar e Ristorante, Spago Maui and DUO, a premium steak and seafood restaurant balance the outstanding culinary offerings. This sophisticated home away from home caters to the needs and interests of all generations—offering world-class activities and one-of-a-kind *Unforgettable Events*, sports and cultural events not experienced elsewhere.

In addition, Four Seasons Resort Maui at Wailea has partnered with Hawaiian Legacy Hardwoods (HLH), in an effort to reforest native koa trees on the slopes of Mauna Kea. Located 34 miles north of Hilo, Hawaii, above the historic Umikoa Village, HLH is donating 1000 acres of land toward achieving a sustainable tropical forest. Once the personal property of King Kamehameha I, old growth koa is being used as the seed source to return the forest to its former glory. The Four Seasons Resort Maui is also working on an ongoing corporate initiative to plant 10 million trees. Within this initiative, the property's employees have made several trips to the neighboring island of Kahoolawe in reforestation efforts. The total of trees on Maui and Kahoolawe planted by the resort is upwards of 4000.

There is no resort fee and a multitude of complimentary services and amenities are provided to all resort guests.

www.fourseasons.com/maui | Tel: 1 808 874 8000

Pickled Mango Sundae

Preparation: 2 hours | Serves: 15

Ingredients:

Mango Ice Cream:
3-2/3 cup mango purée
1-1/3 cup sugar
1/2 cup glucose powder
2 tsp sorbet stabilizer
10 oz water

Ice Cream Base:
1 qt ml milk
4 oz cream
9 egg yolks
1 cup sugar
3 oz liquid glucose

Frozen Lime Yogurt:
2 qts plain yogurt
7-1/2 oz corn syrup
2-1/3 cup glucose powder
3 lime zest
juice of 1 lime

Pickled Mango:
4 cups sugar
4 cups white distilled vinegar
1 tbsp Hawaiian Salt
2 tbsp Li Hing Mui Powder*
7-10 pc green mango
18 pc Li Hing Mui seeds*

Ginger Syrup:
7 oz fresh ginger, peeled and sliced
1 qt water
3 tbsp Maui honey
juice of 1 lemon
4-3/4 lb sugar
4-1/4 cups glucose powder

continued...

FIVE STAR RECIPES FROM WORLD FAMOUS HOTELS & RESORTS

Pickled Mango Sundae

Method:

Ice Cream Base:
Prep: 20 minutes

- Bring the milk, cream and glucose to a boil.
- Whisk together the yolks and sugar. Whisk some of the hot milk into the yolks to equalize temperature and consistency. Return to the pot, and cook over a medium heat until it coats the back of a spoon.
- Strain immediately into another bowl, and place over a second bowl of ice water.
- Stir to lower the temperature and stop cooking. Once cool, cover and place in the refrigerator overnight.

Mango Ice Cream:
Prep: 30 minutes

- Bring water, sugar, glucose and stabilizer to a boil. Cool overnight then add the mango puree.
- Measure equal quantities mango base and ice cream base (1 quart to 1 quart).
- Freeze in an ice cream machine according to manufacturer's instructions.

Frozen Lime Yogurt:
Prep: 20 minutes

- Combine all ingredients and freeze in ice cream machine.

Pickled Mango:
3 days prior - Prep: 40 minutes

- Boil all ingredients together except the mango. Cool liquid to room temperature.
- Peel and slice green mango, divide into 3 containers.
- Add 6 pc of Li Hing Mui seed to each container and fill to the top with the cooled liquid.
- Store in the refrigerator for at least 3 days before use.

Ginger Syrup:
Prep: 20 minutes

- Boil ginger and water together. Remove from heat and allow to steep for as long as possible to get the best flavor.
- Add in the honey and lemon juice, then the sugar and glucose, and bring to a boil. (Use a high sided pot as it will boil over.)
- Simmer for 5 minutes and remove from the heat. Check thickness on a cold plate. It should be the consistency of honey when cold.
- Cool and refrigerate.

Assembly:

- Freeze the glasses. Remove from the freezer and dip rim in Li Hang Maui powder (condensation on the glass will catch the powder).
- Spoon a little mango purée inside and swirl around the glass.
- Place some cubed fresh mango and a little cubed pickled mango in the glass.
- Top with a scoop of frozen lime yogurt and repeat layering yogurt with fresh and pickled mango.
- Top with a scoop of mango ice cream.
- Pipe in a little whipped cream, and put on the fresh mango fan and streusel crumble**.
- Add on a little more pickled mango.
- Place ginger syrup in a small dish so each guest can pour on as desired.

Li Hang Maui powder and seeds come from the Hawaiian Li Hang mud seed (dried plums) and is also sprinkled on fruit, crackers and popcorn.

** See Recipe Basics.

RECIPE BASICS

Recipe Basics

Substitution for Bisquick

1 cup flour
1- 1/2 tsp baking powder
1/4 tsp
1 tbsp shortening, oil, or melted butter

- Sift and mix the dry ingredients together using a whisk or fork.
- Evenly cut the shortening or oil into the dry mixture.
- Mix well and store in an air-tight container in a dry place. It will keep for 3-4 months. If using melted butter, store in fridge.

Phyllo Cups

If you are unable to find the right size phyllo cups in your grocery store freezer, you can easily make them at home. They can be baked in advance and kept in an air tight container for about 5-7 days and leftovers can be wrapped tightly and stored in the freezer for a couple of months. They can be filled with all sorts of tasty tidbits for desserts, brunch and the mini size is great for hors' doeuvres.

1 package frozen phyllo dough (2 rolls) thawed
1/2 cup melted butter
white sugar
oil spray

- Preheat oven to 375°F. Spray muffin or tart baking tins lightly with oil spray.
- Take one sheet of phyllo, brush with melted butter, then sprinkle lightly with sugar. Lay a second sheet on top and repeat the process until you have a stack of five sheets.
- Cut into small equal squares and press into cups. Bake about 10 minutes or until they are a light golden brown. Watch carefully to be sure they do not burn. Remove from oven and carefully twist the cups out of the pans. Makes about 25 to 100 cups, depending upon size.

Puff Pastry

It is important to note that puff pastry and phyllo dough are not the same thing and create different results. It is best not to substitute one for the other. Several companies make first-rate frozen puff pastry shells and sheets which you can find at your local market. Just be sure to read the package carefully as they both may come in similar packaging.

If you prefer to make your own puff pastry, it does take time and patience but it is not very difficult. To successfully make and use it, you need to know what puff pastry is and how it works. There are only four ingredients: flour, unsalted butter, salt, and water. There is no leavening agent of any kind. It is the way the ingredients are combined that causes the dough rise and become so airy.

Puff pastry expands at least 7-8 times its unbaked thickness. It is important to take your time and wait the recommended time chilling thoroughly between turns so that the layers puff up when baked.

Recipe Basics

2 cups all-purpose flour
1/2 lb (2 sticks) at room temperature
1/2 tsp salt
1/2 cup cold water

- Mix the flour and salt together in a large bowl or in the bowl of a stand mixer with a dough hook. Gradually stir in water, using the dough hook or a wooden spoon, until the dough holds together and does not stick to the sides of the bowl. Use only enough water to reach this consistency. Cover the bowl and chill in the fridge for 20 minutes.
- Using a pastry blender, roughly cut the butter into thumb-size chunks.
- Place the butter chunks between two pieces of plastic wrap and pound into a flat disc using a rolling pin or other heavy object. Refrigerate about 20 minutes or until firm.
- On a lightly floured surface, roll out the dough into a large rectangle about 1/3 inch thick. Gently dust away any excess flour on the dough surface.
- Place the chilled butter disc in the center, folding the two ends of the dough over the disc is so it completely encased. Be sure no butter pokes through the dough. Now fold the dough into thirds—the first "turn." Rotate the dough 90 degrees and roll out again into rectangle again, about 1/3 inch thick, and fold into thirds. Wrap in plastic wrap and refrigerate for at least 30 minutes. Repeat this process two more times for a total of 6 turns, being sure to chill the dough in the fridge for at least 30 minutes between each procedure.
- When done, wrap dough tightly in plastic wrap refrigerate overnight. The dough is now ready to use in any recipe calling for puff pastry.

Caster Sugar

Caster sugar is a British term for very fine granulated sugar. Because the crystals are so minute, they dissolve very quickly and are particularly useful in meringues, custards, and mousses, baking and sweetening cold drinks and cocktails. It may not be easy to find but it is very easy to make.

Granulated sugar—a little more than the recipe calls for.

- Place the sugar in a food processor or blender and pulse 1-2 minutes until it reaches a super-fine, but not too powdery, consistency. Be sure to cover the top with a cloth or lid to keep the dust in the processor.
- Allow the sugar to settle for a few minutes. Then, use in place of the caster sugar called for in your recipe.
- If you are concerned about the sugar etching a blender container made of plastic, use a coffee or spice grinder instead.

Clarified Butter

Milk solids cause butter to burn quickly in cooking. By removing them, you are able to cook meats, fish and other foods with butter at higher temperatures for longer periods of time, making it perfect for pan frying. It's also the milk solids that cause butter to become rancid. By removing them, the clarified butter will keep in a tightly sealed container in the fridge for about a month. The process takes about 15 minutes and yields about 2/3 cup.

Recipe Basics

2 sticks (1/2 lb) unsalted butter, cut into small pieces

- Place the butter in the saucepan and melt slowly over low heat. Do not stir or rush this process.
- When thorough melted, remove from the heat. Let stand for 5 minutes. Skim the foam off the top and slowly pour through a mesh cloth or fine strainer into a container. Discard the milky solids in the bottom of pan or strainer.

Four Spice Recipe

1 tbsp white pepper
1 tsp grated nutmeg
1 tsp ground ginger
1/2 tsp ground cloves

- Mix well together and store in air-tight container in a dry place.

Pickled Ginger (Gari)

8 oz fresh ginger root, peeled
1-1/2 tsp sea salt
1 cup rice vinegar, unseasoned
1/3 cup white sugar
1 Thai chili pepper (optional)
1/4 tsp whole peppercorns
2 whole cloves

- Slice the ginger into very thin slices. Place in a bowl* and sprinkle with the salt. Toss well to coat. Let stand for about 30 minutes. Transfer to a clean jar or other container with a tight-fitting lid.
- In a saucepan, stir the rice vinegar, peppercorns, cloves, Thai chili and sugar together until the sugar has dissolved. Bring to a boil, then simmer for 5 minutes. Strain and pour over the ginger slices in the jar.
- Allow the mixture to cool, then put the lid on the container and store in the fridge for up to 2 weeks. Liquid may turn pink.

   * *Do not use a metallic container of any kind.*

Gelatin Sheets and Powder

Gelatin is an odorless, tasteless thickening agent made of collagen produced from animal bones and other parts which, when heated, melts, and when thoroughly cooled, regains a jellied consistency. It comes in the form of sheets, also called leaves, and powder and is used primarily in desserts, candy, and aspics as well as jam, jelly, yogurt, some margarines and is often added to low-fat foods to add volume without increasing the calorie count.

Recipe Basics

Professional cooks generally prefer the sheet/leaf variety because the gelatin is clearer, easy to use, and there is no chance of undissolved granules. You can also substitute one form for the other—1 tbsp powdered gelatin equals 3 sheets of leaf gelatin—but try to use the form specified in the recipe and carefully follow the package directions.

"Bloom" is a term referring to the process of softening the gelatin sheets in water or other liquid prior to melting them. It also refers to the firmness of the sheet which determines the grade of the gelatin. The higher the bloom, the higher the cost. The most popular are Silver and Gold grades.

If you cannot find gelatin sheets or leaves in your local gourmet mart, there are a number of sources on the Internet. Knox is the most common powdered form, but other brands are also easily found online.

For vegan and kosher requirements, substitutions with similar properties to gelatin include agar-agar, which comes from seaweed; xanthan gum., a gluten-free, corn-based product; and pectin, a natural plant-based product.

Garlic Confit

For garlic lovers, garlic confit is no stranger. It's handy to keep in the fridge for pasta and other sauces, topping pizza, making garlic mashed potatoes, herb and guacamole dips and much more. Add a bit of the oil to mashed potatoes for quick garlic mashed potatoes.

3 cups unpeeled garlic cloves (about 100-125 cloves)
3 cups extra virgin olive oil

- Fill a large bowl with cold water and a few ice cubes and set aside
- Bring 2 quarts of water to a fast boil in a medium saucepan. Place the unpeeled garlic cloves in a sieve or strainer and dip them in the hot water for about 20 seconds to loosen the skins. Remove the sieve of cloves from the boiling water and dip in the ice water. When the cloves are cooled, place on a cutting surface, remove root ends, and the skins should slip right off. Pat dry with clean paper towels.
- Place the peeled garlic cloves in a heavy, medium-sized saucepan. Add the oil, covering the cloves by 1/2 inch. Adjust the amount of oil as needed.
- Heat the pan over a medium heat and as soon as it begins to bubble, reduce heat to the lowest setting on your stove: It should not exceed 220°F. As the oil heats, fragments of skin might surface. Using a mesh utensil, skim them off.
- Carefully cook the cloves for about 40-45 minutes, stirring occasionally to avoid browning. When it becomes very tender, the garlic becomes a light golden color. Remove the pan from heat and set aside. Allow the cloves to cool in the oil.
- Store in an airtight container and refrigerate for up to one week. Always bring the confit to room temperature before using and use a clean spoon to remove the garlic. Makes 4 cups.

Recipe Basics

Stock vs. Broth

There is a definite difference between stock and broth. Stock, which is made with meaty bones, has a richer flavor and heartier body due to the gelatin released as the bones simmer. Broth, made mainly from meat—no bones — has a lighter essence.

Chicken Stock

For a hearty, flavorful stock, this basic recipe has lots of flavor.

1-1/2 lbs meaty chicken bones—wings, backs, whole carcass, legs, thighs
1 celery stalk, halved
1 medium carrot, cleaned and halved
1 small onion, halved
1/2 head of garlic
3 stems of fresh parsley
3 stems of fresh thyme (optional)
6-8 peppercorns
salt to taste
2 qts water

- Place all the ingredients in a stock pot and cover with the water.
- Bring to a simmer and cook for at least 4-8 hours, the longer the better to maximize the flavor.
- When done, add the salt to taste.
- Strain the liquid through a fine sieve into an air tight container and discard all the solids. Stock can be stored in the fridge for up to 5 days.

If you are short on time, you can use canned chicken broth and simmer it in a pot with onion, garlic, carrots, celery —anything but pungent vegetables such as broccoli, cauliflower or turnips, plus a couple of bay leaves, salt and a few peppercorns. The longer it simmers, the stronger the flavor. It is an acceptable substitute, but it is not the same as homemade.

White Lamb Stock

The following is Dromoland Castle Executive Chef David McCann's recipe for preparing the stock used in his Dromoland Irish Stew.

8- l/2 qts water
4-3/4 lbs raw lamb bones
2 carrots
2 medium onions
3 celery sticks
2 bay leaves
5 cloves garlic
10 black peppercorns

Recipe Basics

- Put the bones in a large stock pot, cover with water and bring to a boil. Skim well and reduce to a simmer. Continue cooking for 1 hour, skimming occasionally.
- Peel and wash all the vegetables, keeping them whole. Add to the stock with the herbs, peppercorns and garlic.
- Bring back to a boil, skim well and reduce to a simmer. Cook for 3 hours.
- Put the stock through a fine sieve, cool, and refrigerate or freeze in air tight containers. Makes about 5 quarts.

Roasted Tomato Sauce

olive oil
2 lbs fresh tomatoes
8 cloves garlic, peeled and minced (optional)
4 tbsp unsalted butter
1 tsp Kosher salt
freshly ground black pepper

- Heat the oven to 350°F. Line a 9x13-inch baking dish with aluminium foil. Coat the foil with an oil spray or lightly rub with olive oil.
- Chop the tomatoes evenly and spread them in the baking dish. Stir in the minced garlic, a drizzle of olive oil, and 1 tsp of salt (or to taste) and freshly ground black pepper. Cut the butter into small cubes and distribute evenly over the tomatoes.
- Bake the tomatoes 2 to 3 hours. The timing is flexible, depending upon your desired outcome. You can bake them until the tomatoes just begin to break down and release their juices, or you can continue baking up to 3 hours or until their edges blacken and the juices are reduced significantly.
- Store in the fridge in an airtight container for several days and/or freeze unused portions for future uses. Makes about 2-1/2 cups.

Crispy Streusel Crumble

1 cup flour
1/2 cup brown sugar, packed
1/2 tsp salt
1 rounded tsp cinnamon
1/2 tsp nutmeg or giner
1 stick unsalted butter, cut into small pieces
2/3 cup chopped walnuts, pecans or almonds (optional)

- Mix well together all the dry ingredients.
- Cut in the butter pieces and keep mixing gently with your hands until it becomes crumbly. If using nuts, add in and mix at this time and mix well.
- Place on a baking sheet and bake in a 375° F oven, stirring mixture as necessary, until golden brown.

This recipe Is also tasty as a pre-cooked topping for fruit desserts.

Add to muffins, pies or pastries before cooking. Unused portion can be frozen. This recipe makes enough topping for one pie or one batch of muffins. Double recipe for the Pickled Mango Sundae recipe on page 111.

Metric Measurement Conversions

METRIC MEASUREMENT CONVERSIONS

Below are some basic conversions to help those who want to translate U.S. measurements into metric. Amounts are rounded off for easy measurement. If you have further questions, we have listed a few useful online conversion sites at the end of this section.

Approximate Fluid Equivalents:

1/2 tsp	2-1/2 ml
1 tsp	5 ml
1 tbsp	15 ml
1/4 cup	60 ml
1/3 cup	80 ml
1/2 cup	120 ml
2/3 cup	158 ml
3/4 cup	178 ml
1 cup	240 ml
1-1/2 cups	355 ml
2 cups	480 ml
1 pt	480 ml
1 qt	1 liter	960 ml

Approximate Weight Equivalents:

1 oz	28 g
4 oz	1/4 lb	114 g
1/3 lb	150 g
8 oz	1/2 lb	227 g
2/3 lb	300 g
12 oz	3/4 lb	340 g
16 oz	1 lb	454 g
2 lb	907 g

Handy Websites with Conversion Calculators:

www.onlineconversion.com/weight_volume_cooking.htm

www.metric-conversions.org/volume/us-ounces-to-liters.htm

www.checkyourmath.com/convert/weight_mass/lb_kg.php

www.jsward.com/cooking/conversion.shtml

www.bariatriccookery.com/metric-conversion-chart

www.convertMetricequivalenttunits.com/from/2+lbs/to/kg

METRIC MEASUREMENT CONVERSIONS

Approximate By Ingredient:

Flour:

All-Purpose, sifted:

1 tbsp	5 g
1/4 cup	25 g
1/3 cup	30 g
1/2 cup	50 g
2/3 cup	65 g
3/4 cup	70 g
1 cup	95 g

All-Purpose, unsifted:

1 tbsp	5 g
1/4 cup	31 g
1/3 cup	42 g
1/2 cup	63 g
2/3 cup	75 g
3/4 cup	85 g
1 cup	125 g

Sugar:

Granulated:

1 tbsp	15 g
1/4 cup	50 g
1/3 cup	70 g
1/2 cup	100 g
2/3 cup	135 g
3/4 cup	150 g
1 cup	200 g

Sugar Continued:

Powdered:

1 tbsp	10 g
1/4 cup	40 g
1/3 cup	55 g
1/2 cup	80 g
2/3 cup	105 g
3/4 cup	120 g
1 cup	160 g

Brown, packed:

1 oz	27 g
1/2 cup | 4 oz	110 g
1 cup | 8 oz	220 g

Butter, Margarine, Fats, Cheese:

1 tbsp	15 g
1/4 cup	57 g
3-1/2 oz	100 g
1/2 cup	115 g
1 cup	228 g

METRIC MEASUREMENT CONVERSIONS

Approximate By Ingredient:

Milk and Cream:

1 tbsp	15 ml
2 oz | 1/4 cup	60 ml
2-1/2 oz | 1/3 cup	80 ml
4 oz | 1/2 cup	120 ml
5-1/2 oz | 2/3 cup	160 ml
6 oz | 3/4 cup	180 ml
8 oz | 1 cup	236 ml

Honey & Syrups:

1 tbsp	21 g
1/4 cup	85 g
1/3 cup	113 g
1/2 cup	170 g
1 cup	340 g

Nuts:

1 oz	28 g
4 oz	113 g
8 oz	227 g
16 oz | 1 lb	454 g

Rice, uncooked:

1/4 cup	48 g
1/3 cup	65 g
1/2 cup	95 g
2/3 cup	125 g
3/4 cup	140 g
1 cup	190 g

Vegetables, chopped, minced:

1 tbsp	3 g
1/4 cup	49 g
1/3 cup	65 g
1 cup	236 g
1 lb	453 g

Meats:

1/2 lb	226 g
1/3 lb	150 g
1 lb	453 g
2 lbs	907 g

Farenheit to Celsius:

212 F	100 C
225 F	107 C
250 F	120 C
275 F	135 C
300 F	150 C
325 F	160 C
350 F	180 C
375 F	190 C
400 F	205 C
425 F	218 C
450 F	235 C
475 F	245 C
500 F	260 C

Index by Recipe
Index by Hotel/Resort

Index by Recipe

Breakfast & Brunch
Bea's Eggs Royale *17*
Stamp & Go *19*
German Apple Pancake *21*
Salmon Scrambled Eggs *23*

Appetizers, Soups & Salads
Prawn and Lobster Cocktail *27*
Cheese Straws and Spiced Nuts *29*
Chicken Liver Pâté *31*
Bea's Chicken Soup *33*
Celeriac Soup *35*
Creek Beet Salad *37*
BT's Cabbage Salad *39*
Kikorangi Blue Cheese, Pear & Vanilla Salad *41*

Meats
Dromoland Irish Stew *45*
Lamb in Puff Pastry *47*
Hand Chopped Sirloin *49*
Roast Loin of Dorset Lamb *51*
Braised Leg of Lamb *55*

Poultry
Jerk Chicken *59*
Duck Cottage Pie *61*
Arthur's Chicken Curry *63*
Sesame Fried Chicken *65*
Duckling Filet *67*
Organic Chicken with Pearl Barley *69*

Index by Recipe

Fish

Poached Ahi with Apple Fennel Salad *73*
Lobster Palm Heart with Papaya Coulis *75*
Wild Sea Bass with Grilled Vegetables and Foamed Lobster Sauce *77*
Roast Monk Fish, Potatoes and Peas *79*
Prawn Stroganoff *81*
King Lobster *83*
Dover Sole *85*
Glazed Turbot with Glazed Peas 'André Moreau' *87*

Pasta

Vegetarian Cannelloni with Frisée Salad *91*
Pasta Prima Vera *93*
Tuna Spaghetti *95*

Desserts

Rice Pudding *99*
Parfait Vanilla Mousse with Cantaloupe *101*
Crème Caramel with Mango *103*
Honeycomb Ice Cream *105*
Summer Strawberry Crumble *107*
Bea's Cheesecake *109*
Pickled Mango Sundae *111*

Index by Hotel/Resort

'41, London, England
Cheese Straws and Spiced Nuts *29*

Acorn Inn, Dorset, England
BT's Cabbage Salad *39*

Hotel d'Angleterre, Geneva, Switzerland
Hand Chopped Sirloin *49*

Ashford Castle, County Mayo, Ireland
Rice Pudding *99*

Ballyfin, County Laois, Ireland
Organic Chicken with Pearl Barley *69*
Summer Strawberry Crumble *107*

Blantyre, Lenox, Massachusetts, USA
Celeriac Soup *35*

Bushmans Kloof, Western Cape, South Africa
Sesame Fried Chicken *65*

The Chesterfield Mayfair, London, England
Dover Sole *85*
Honeycomb Ice Cream *105*

The Chesterfield Palm Beach, Florida, USA
Prawn and Lobster Cocktail *27*

Dromoland Castle, County Clare, Ireland
Dromoland Irish Stew *45*
Roast Monk Fish, Potatoes and Peas *79*
Crème Caramel with Mango *103*

The Duke of Richmond Hotel, Guernsey, England
Prawn Stroganoff *81*

The Egerton House Hotel, London, England
Bea's Chicken Soup *33*

FIVE STAR RECIPES FROM WORLD FAMOUS HOTELS & RESORTS

Index by Hotel/Resort

Four Seasons Resort Maui at Wailea, Maui, Hawaii
Poached Ahi with Apple Fennel Salad *73*
Pickled Mango Sundae *111*

GoldenEye Resort, Oracabessa Bay, Jamaica
Stamp & Go *19*
Jerk Chicken *59*

Hotel Le Toiny, St Barth, Caribbean
Duckling Filet *67*

Hotel Lungarno, Florence, Italy
Parfait Vanilla Mousse with Cantaloupe *101*

Inn at 202 Dover, Talbot County, Maryland, USA
German Apple Pancake *21*

Lodge at Kauri Cliffs, Matauri Bay, New Zealand
Kikorangi Blue Cheese, Pear & Vanilla Salad *41*

The Milestone, London, England
Bea's Eggs Royale *17*

The Montague on the Gardens, London, England
Lamb in Puff Pastry *47*
Tuna Spaghetti *95*

The Old Government House Hotel and Spa, Guernsey, England
Pasta Prima Vera *93*

The Oyster Box, Kwa-Zulu Natal, South Africa
Arthur's Chicken Curry *63*

Palazzo Avino, Ravello, Amalfi Coast, Italy
King Lobster *83*

Ranch at Rock Creek, Philipsburg, Montana, USA
Creek Beet Salad *37*
Braised Leg of Lamb *55*

Index by Hotel/Resort

Regent Berlin, Berlin, Germany
Wild Sea Bass with Grilled Vegetables and Foamed Lobster Sauce *77*

Summer Lodge, Dorset, England
Roast Loin of Dorset Lamb *51*
Duck Cottage Pie *61*

Terre Blanche, Provence, France
Glazed Turbot with Glazed Peas 'André Moreau' *87*

The Twelve Apostles Hotel and Spa, Cape Town, South Africa
Bea's Cheesecake *109*

Viceroy Bali, Ubud, Bali
Salmon Scrambled Eggs *23*
Lobster Palm Heart with Papaya Coulis *75*
Vegetarian Cannelloni with Frisée Salad *91*

ABOUT THE AUTHOR

Linda Lang is currently travel editor for Westlake Magazine, a premier upscale Southern California lifestyle publication.

For over three decades, she has stayed in the world's most luxurious hotels, dined in their fine restaurants, met with chefs, and watched gastronomy evolve into a major part of the travel experience. In FIVE STAR RECIPES FROM WORLD FAMOUS HOTELS AND RESORTS— the first volume in her new Taste of Travel series, she shares recipes, photos and presentations of the stunning properties that offer them.

Linda has traveled the Orient Express from Istanbul to Paris, seen bird's-eye views of the French countryside from hot air balloons, walked the cobbled streets of medieval villages and avenues of the world's great cities, and snorkeled in the clear waters of the Caribbean, Mexico, Tahiti, and Hawai'i.

She has also authored two eBooks -- THE PARTY PLANNER and EASY PARTY RECIPES, both available on Amazon.com.

The next volume in her Taste of Travel series is scheduled for release early next year. Her blog can be found at LindaLangsTasteofTravel.com.

Made in the USA
Lexington, KY
17 December 2016